Seeing the EXTRAORDINARY *in the* ORDINARY

Lessons in Hope and Healing

HEATHER DURENBERGER

Wisdom
Editions
Minneapolis

Minneapolis

FIRST EDITION DECEMBER 2015

SEEING THE EXTRAORDINARY IN THE ORDINARY:

Lessons in Hope and Healing

Copyright © 2015 by Heather Durenberger

Printed in the United States of America.

10 9 8 7 6 5 4 3 2 1

Cover and interior design: Gary Lindberg

ISBN: 978-1-939548-38-2

Seeing the
EXTRAORDINARY
in the
ORDINARY

Lessons in Hope and Healing

HEATHER DURENBERGER

To my children David Paul, Jacob, Hope and Amelia.
May you always see the extraordinary in the ordinary
and may you continue to reflect God's love and light in
all that you do.

Love you mostest,
Mom

Be still, and know that I am God
Be still, and know that I am
Be still, and know
Be still
Be

Psalm 46:10

This scripture serves as my invitation to stop, breathe and reflect in the midst of a crazy, busy world. My journey began here learning to slow down, taking a breath, and beginning to notice the divine in my day.

Contents

Gratitudes

Here are a few key people who were very important in helping me to weave together this book from a collection of stories and experiences.

My Heavenly Father, who has given me a unique combination of talents and life experiences that at times seem unconnected and strange, but as they weave together into this tapestry of life, I feel compelled and privileged to share them with the world. So my first thank you is to the One who loves me like crazy and His ability to show up in my day exactly when I need Him. I am grateful that He knows me by name and counts every hair on my head (which is a lot!) Thank You for loving me enough to push me outside my comfort zone to share Your love and light with others. Amen.

My publisher Gary Lindberg, whose mission for publishing books is to make our world and the people in it a more loving and peaceful place. I am extremely grateful for his belief in me and the love and light I hope to be and reflect in this world.

My personal coach, Dr. Lynn Nodland, for her wisdom and for loving me enough to coach me into my potential. I can honestly say this book would not have happened without her faithfully holding me accountable and coaching me to say "No" to certain activities in my life, so I could say "Yes" to this book.

On a personal note, my wonderful children, David Paul, Jacob, Hope and Amelia who are constantly teaching me about what it means to be courageous, gracious and truly reflections of God's deep love for each of us. I am so grateful for each of them and their support in writing this book.

And finally, my dear husband who serves as my safe harbor during storms and pushes me to be my best during times of calm. Dearest David, you are truly a gift given from above and I treasure and adore you, always. Your unwavering belief grounds me and fills me with courage and confidence as I step into this next evolution of work. I couldn't and wouldn't do it without you babe!

About the Author

Heather Durenberger is a consultative coach, instructor, public speaker, and author. Her favorite quote is a proverb: "If your vision is for a year, plant wheat. If your vision is for ten years, plant trees. If your vision is for a lifetime, plant people." Heather is passionate about planting people by meeting them where they are, guiding self-discovery, insights and growth to unlock their fullest potential.

She is a graduate level instructor at the UniverSt. Mary's University of Minnesota in the Human Development and the Philanthropy Department. Heather consults and coaches leadership teams in addition to public speaking. As a lifelong learner, she has a master of business administration and a master of biopsychology, not to mention a house full of books! Her most cherished title is wife and proud mom of four children.

You can reach Heather on her website at heatherdurenberger.com.

Foreword

Lift up your head and heart. Find the extraordinary in the ordinary.

This is a collection of experiences I have gathered from my life journey. Until recently I only shared these stories with my family and friends. However, I have since found that sharing them with a larger audience opens a door for others to see how God is working in their daily lives. I offer you these stories to help you to *see* more… to help you to *be* more… to help you to be all that God dreams for you to be.

As a minister's daughter, I assumed that all kids grew up in the same kind of chaos that I did. From the time I could walk and talk, I was part of an amazing family—my church family. Actually my amazing family was even larger than my church family because it was made up of the larger community in which I lived. From a young age I saw the most incredible human stories unfold among these 'family' members.

As a preacher's kid I often was invited into people's homes and lives. I was able to experience many incredible moments with them. From happy births to devastating deaths and unimaginable betrayals, I have experienced life-changing, faith changing moments as an honored observer. These moments have strengthened and challenged my faith as well as broadened my thinking and feeling beyond what I even knew they could be. I have come to realize how precious life is and how quickly life can change. I have come to realize how different people see different truths. My faith is not only in my Heavenly Father, but also in my fellow human beings.

The stories and perspectives I share here are mine, but please understand that there can be many sides to a story. All of us see and experience the world through many lenses. I fully own my personal biases, so I ask you for grace and patience as I relate my stories and observations to you. Like everyone's journey, mine is a work in progress. I am still becoming who I was made to be. And so I humbly offer a glimpse of some memorable times in which I felt close to the Divine and had such wonderful, sometimes terrifying, but always faith-deepening experiences.

I hope through my stories you might develop a greater awareness of God's presence in your daily life. As scripture tells us in Psalm 23, He walks with us through the valleys and He walks with us on the mountain tops. Each of us moves forward on our faith journey on a path that is unique to us. Having a greater sense of our connection to the Almighty and knowing His consistent presence in our daily lives gives us nourishment for our journey.

Are you open to God's presence in your life? Do you hear His gentle tapping on your heart? Or like me, does it sometimes take a two-by-four across the back of the head to get your attention? As I look back at my life experiences I am trying to learn to be more sensitive and more aware of God's presence in my daily, ordinary (most of the time) life.

My prayer for you is that you may come to see, feel and know God's presence in the ordinary. For it is in the ordinary that God truly works His most incredible miracles. Look and see. Begin to notice what is at work in your life and you will be truly amazed and never be the same.

This book is all about you, the reader. My primary goal is for you to think differently after reading these pages than when you started reading this book. I know that is a tall order. I will have to get your attention, engage you, motivate you, inspire you, educate you, and then instill in you a sense of personal accountability to nurture your new way of thinking.

Two ah-ha moments from my personal journey have helped shaped my professional work. Back in

2004 I was serving on several boards and was chairing some committees. I was the mother of a three-year-old and an eighteen-month-old. And I was expecting a third child.

I can vividly remember walking into an American Indian food shelf in Minneapolis to deliver some donations. I can remember the acrid smell in the air from the Indian practice of smudging. As I was finishing my business, I turned to see a very young woman with a very unhappy newborn baby. I quickly learned that this mom was completely out of formula and diapers and the food shelf did not have the appropriate kind of formula and was short on diapers.

I remember finding a bench and slouching down on it for a moment. I felt deflated. I felt tired. I actually cried in public. Here I was volunteering to the max, giving everything I had to give, and yet it still wasn't enough for those who I had committed to serve. My two hands were limiting me. The manner in which I was volunteering was limiting me. I needed to think differently about how to serve.

Two months later my father passed away unexpectedly. At sixty-four he had given everything, including his health, to his ministry as a Presbyterian pastor. As my family arrived to manage his estate, we walked into his apartment and found it exactly as he had left it. His cane was by the door, his shoes lined up ready to be worn—everything was waiting for him. We began to unpack and get ready for the work of organizing his things and settling his affairs.

We were all spinning in grief, but then my brother found a hidden treasure that lifted us up. In my dad's Bible was my business card marking Chapter 25 in the Book of Matthew. This Chapter is about the importance of using your talents to minister to those who are lonely, hungry, sick and imprisoned. It encourages us to make the most of our God-given talents.

Wow. I had been struggling with how to work differently. Here, in my darkness and valley of grief, came an answer to prayer. I needed to shift my work from direct service to helping leaders. By working as a catalyst and coach, I could multiply my impact on the lives of those I sought to serve. I suddenly had an insight into how I could make better use of my unique gifts.

You see, I just love to serve. Ever since I was little girl following after my daddy in his parish ministry I have been involved with serving: from board service, to direct service, to volunteer recruitment and volunteer management; from hospital visitation to book drives; from fundraisers to friend raisers; from politics to church to community boards to PTOs. I just love to serve.

My life has been about serving others in the nonprofit space. From this service, I have come to learn what it takes to survive and thrive in the world of nonprofits. From this service, I have been rewarded with passion, energy, and an understanding that I can be part of something bigger than myself. Nonprofit service or ministry is a demanding profession. It challenges and pushes you further that you think is possible, but in the end the rewards are hard to put into words.

I stand in awe of those engaged in nonprofit work. This includes a wide segment of our population who serve as board members, volunteers, executive directors and staff. I know the passion and energy you bring with you every day, including many weeknights and weekends. We get the privilege of seeing people at their best and at their worst or most vulnerable.

Your commitment to serve is what fuels my work. So sit back and dive into some of the extraordinary miracles I have had the privilege to witness. For I believe that God is still in the miracle business. If you slow down, you too will notice and experience the extraordinary in the ordinary.

Did You See It?

On the evening of our 10th wedding anniversary, my husband and I were heading to the dining room for dinner. As I looked up at the sky, I saw the most amazing double rainbow over the Atlantic Ocean. I mentioned to my husband, as I probably have hundreds of times, that rainbows remind me God always keeps his promises. And this time, I thought, God must really mean it because there were two glorious rainbows arching over the sky.

As we arrived at the dinner table I asked those who had already gathered if they had noticed the amazing dual rainbows in the sky. They had not. They had rushed to the dining room with their eyes glued to the path and had missed them. Immediately they rose and ran to a window to catch a glimpse, but by this time the rainbows were fading, and they could only see a fragment of one of the rainbows. They had missed the natural masterpiece, the glorious sight.

How many times in our rush to *do* have we missed seeing something beautiful and amazing? Whether it is connecting with a stranger or with someone who could really use our presence that day, we missed it.

I encourage you to slow down. Give yourself more time to pause, look around, and discover what you may have otherwise missed. Notice your spouse and children. See them. Begin to be more aware of those around you. See the hand of God at work in the world and your life. Then be prepared to be awed, amazed and humbled!

The Open Window

I just love the saying *when life closes a door God always opens a window*. But how many of us stubbornly stand behind the door and never have the courage to go and find the open window?

When life happens, as it always does, we must have courage to leave what we have known and be open to what is next. For most of us this takes immense courage because, like me, perhaps you have been hurt deeply many times. But it is in this hurt that we can become highly motivated, maybe for the first time in a long time, to do something different for a change.

So when life closes a door, be brave, honor the hurt, and then step away from the closed door and find your open window. I have seen people do this many times. It is beautiful and powerful. And I never fail to admire the courage it takes.

The Hamster Wheel

In our world of super-size, super-speed and super-ficial, I would like to offer you the chance to pause. Not many people choose to stop on their own. The reason we stop is because of physical or emotional pain. Resting is usually due to illness or loss. This is an open invitation for you to stop without the pain, loss or heartache.

For many of us the world is on automatic. We continue to do as many of those before us have done. We keep going through the same routines, same motions, and same old lives because that is what we expect and know—and because it is expected of us. It's the "we've always done it that way" kind of thinking.

But here is the deal. We are each uniquely made to do something very special... something that cannot be done like everyone else... something that requires attention... something that speaks to your heart and soul... something that requires you to step off your hamster wheel.

Make and take time to see where you are. Take time to remember where you wanted to be. Then life for you will change—you will change. So I invite you to pause, breathe and begin to be.

I know this is a process. For me it literally took years, so I get it. I believe in baby steps, so maybe you can begin by pausing three minutes a day. Take three minutes to stop and breathe deeply. Take three minutes to remind yourself of who you are and who you hope to be.

I invite you to pause and see what happens.

The Silver Lining

Parker Palmer has a beautiful saying. When something tragic happens you have two choices. You can break *apart* and dissolve into many pieces—or you can break *open*.

When tragedy and loss occurs, how many times do we stop living the way we used to live and open up to how we *might* live and what we *might* become? For something new to begin, something old must die or be removed. From incredible loss comes the opportunity to stop and reflect. Where am I? This may be the realization that you have drifted to a place that you never intended or imagined. This may be an opportunity to dream about where you might be. This may be your first chance to see or notice a gap between your reality and your aspirations, and what opportunity is in front of you?

You have fresh eyes and perhaps a new filter for how you live your life. I encourage you to take full advantage of the opportunity in front of you. Use the brokenness, use those fresh eyes, the hurt, to unleash what's next. If you have reached rock bottom, then push off from the bottom. If your heart is broken into little pieces, find the courage to let the silver lining emerge—because it is there. Trust that you can survive this pain. Lean into the unknown and let what's next begin to emerge.

You're Never Given More Than You Can Handle. It's Just Circumstances

As a child I often heard the old saying that you're never given more than you can handle. Many times as a preacher's daughter I came to doubt this saying, but time after time I was proven wrong. I have seen not only the strength of the human spirit, but more importantly the amazing grace and power of our Heavenly Father who shows us His strength in our weakness. Nothing exhibits this more vividly for me than the story of one family who seemed to have more than their share of challenges and heartbreaks.

I have served in many different capacities in faith communities. One of my most powerful experiences was serving on the Emergency Committee of my church as I was growing up. Like it sounds, you stand ready for any emergency that happens. It often was an unexpected hospitalization during which we supported a family with any of their needs. Life often got most exciting over holiday weekends, especially if the clergy were on vacation. One holiday weekend I received a call stating that one of our church members had been in a bad accident. Could I quickly make my way to the county hospital ICU unit? My dad, who was also our minister, was out of town so visiting and supporting the family fell to the Emergency Committee—*me*!

As a preacher's kid I had been to many hospital rooms and seen more than my share of people in need. But I was not prepared for the state of this young person who had barely survived a very serious car accident. This beautiful young woman was now hooked up to more tubes and machines than you could count. She was badly swollen and barely recognizable. I was at a loss for what to say or do to support this family. I didn't feel equipped for this moment. Why me?

I had often posed this same question to my dad. What do you say to someone hurting so badly? What does one say to a family member who has a loved one with one foot in this world and one foot in the next? Without pause, Dad reminded me that it is always a good idea to invite God into the struggle. In our moments of weakness, we lean on Him and let Him show us the way.

Remembering this, I invited the family to pray. I helped with arrangements for food, care for the children, and other basic needs. As hours turned into days it became apparent that the family's prayers would be answered. This youth was going to survive, but the quality and realities of her life would be very different than what they had been before the accident.

As the girl grew stronger and was released from the ICU, more challenges would surface. Not only was she facing the effects of what we now call a traumatic brain injury and trying to learn to live as a disabled teenager, but her mother was soon diagnosed with cancer.

I thought, *how much more can this family deal with? Why was this happening to them?* I was amazed at the incredible strength and courage of this mother and family. Not only did she keep caring for her child, but she was also fighting for her own life. Through the weeks of treatment and rehabilitation, this mother persevered. I could not believe what I was seeing. I was worn out by this family's ordeal, but day after day, week after week, the girl's mother fought. And through her weakness God was able to support, heal and make whole what was broken.

When life gets tough, when circumstances get

hard, focus on your Heavenly Father. He will provide for you. Don't be limited by what you think is possible. Trust that God can do more than you can ever imagine and then hold tightly onto that. Trust in Him and watch what happens.

Into the Fog

One of my favorite things on a family road trip is driving through a patch of fog. I love how you can be seeing everything around you, and then suddenly losing all visibility except for the light from the headlights and anything directly one foot ahead of you. This must come from growing up in the snow belt of Western New York. You learn at a young age to trust in the road ahead of you and slow down—but never stop. If you stop, the driver or the snow plow behind you might push you off the side of the road.

For those precious moments, I hold tight to the steering wheel and stay the course, trusting the road and my vehicle to deliver me safely through the fog. I find this also to be useful in our daily lives.

In life, when we head into the fog, what is our typical first reaction? Do we immediately trust God and hold tight to his promises, or do we get grumpy?

I tend to get frustrated when I cannot see what is

ahead of me. Rather than being patient and prayerful, I get uncomfortable. I don't like being reminded that I am not in charge. At such times, though, we need to lean on our Heavenly Father to guide us through the fog. Now, after a lot of practice, when I enter a foggy patch I thank God for his faithfulness to me.

Usually.

Romans 8:28 (ESV)

And we know that for those who love God all things work together for good, for those who are called according to his purpose.

Dear Heavenly Father, you are such a good and loving God. Thank you for guiding me and loving me through the fog. Help me to trust you more and lean into living from this place. Less reliance on me and all reliance on your will and ways. Amen.

Help Me in This Moment

Sometimes it's hard to find the words to describe what I have seen and experienced. I am often reminded of God's grace when I see the strength of others during times of great suffering. I have seen heartbreak that is beyond my belief and understanding. I have seen God's great love and grace extended as a lifeline to those who call on Him. I have seen those who believe and rely on Him experience a peace that surpasses understanding.

In the midst of heartbreak and tears, stand firm in your relationship with your Heavenly Father. Trust in Him. Know that He can turn your weeping at night into joy and dancing in the morning.

Dear Heavenly Father, sometimes it feels as though what pains us is bigger than you. This pain seems to define and blind us from believing in tomorrow. Today, we ask that you would enter our wounded hearts and begin to heal and bring peace to us in the places where we suffer and mourn. Help us to shine light where it is dark, both in the world and in ourselves. Amen.

Being Present

My family was sitting around the kitchen table Sunday morning before services. We could always tell if Dad had written his sermon by how talkative he was. This morning he was quiet. Mom was in the kitchen pulling together breakfast. My brother and I were staring each other down and making silly faces as our tummies rumbled hungrily for breakfast. My dad was wearing his cleric's collar. I didn't like the collar. My friends at school teased me that my dad was a priest, which made me an illegitimate child.

Oh, how I hated that collar.

Mom had just put food on the table when the phone rang. *Here we go*, I thought. In our house, it was not a good sign when the phone rang early in the morning or late at night because in an emergency members of the church—even members of the greater community—would call our house rather than the church. This was before cell phones, and everybody knew they could reach my dad at home.

I jumped up from the table and answered the phone, looking right at my dad. I was feeling rambunctious that morning and looked him right in the eye as I said, "City morgue. You kill 'em, we chill 'em." It had sounded funny on TV. Why not try it?

The line went silent.

"Hello," I said into the receiver.

For a moment, there was only silence.

"Hello—is anyone there?"

A man spoke up. His voice was so soft it was as if he had barely enough breath in him to ask, "Is your dad there?"

"Sure," I said, "he's right here."

I passed the phone to my dad. He gave me a look that indicated that we would have a talk later, then the phone and its obnoxious cord traveled into the other room.

At the table we sat silently and we heard Dad say, "Yes… of course. Call the police, I'll be right there."

In our small town folks usually called the pastor before they called for the police or an ambulance. Whether it was a heart attack or someone being arrested—we had heard it all—people always called Dad first, just like this morning.

We knew the drill. Dad would be gone for hours. Life happened every day, no matter what your calendar or schedule said. Life happened.

Dad headed for the door. Poor Mom… another meal left on the table. No breakfast today. Dad asked me, "Heather, do you want to come along? You know the family and can be helpful."

"Sure, Dad," I said.

Dad hung a cross around his neck, which for him was a treasure made out of nails, and grabbed his Bible. We moved quickly to the car, off on another adventure, another experience in the divine.

We drove in silence—over the years I have learned to stay quiet on such drives. He drove fast, but still it seemed like he was in prayer the whole way over. He had always taught me to ask God to prepare us for any difficulties we were about to walk into. In the past I had heard Dad pray for God to protect him on visits like this, to cover him with truth, to guide his tongue and open his heart.

I loved driving in the car with my dad. He was such a character—which I think most people would have a hard time believing after seeing him in the pulpit. He had the perfect blend of strengths to be a pastor, and he could tell a story or embellish one like no one's business. He always knew what to say. With his height and plus-sized frame, which he would quickly augment from all the church dinners, he certainly did have an air of authority and ministerial presence.

I realize now that during our car rides he was pouring into me wisdom and truths. From all these incredible and often harrowing experiences of life, he was helping me gain important life lessons learned and to see the importance of dealing with adversity and challenges.

Of course, I sometimes saw things differently than Dad; I had no choice but to be different. He always said I was a breath of fresh air. I have learned how close life and death are. I have seen people make good choices and bad. I have seen how at one moment a particular choice can have major implications in your life and those of others. And I have witnessed the amazing grace offered to each of us no matter how we screw up. Time after time I have seen the strength of people overcome enormous challenges.

I cherish those drives in the car and hope to share some of the nuggets of wisdom I learned during those rides. For me, those nuggets were life changers. I hope they can help you live your best life.

On that long-ago day our drive finally came to an end at a middle class home with a wide-open front door. Neighbors had already gathered around the house. As we parked, a police car pulled up. Dad put his hands on my shoulders and we walked through the front door.

I could immediately feel the grief, the heartache, the emotional intensity. The anguish was like a fog throughout the entire front room. It was heavy on me and took away my breath. At my young age I didn't have the language to articulate this sense of foreboding—I just knew deep inside that something terrible had happened here.

I saw a woman on a couch sobbing with her hands on her head—the kind of sobs that make no sound but are so deep that your whole body shakes. A man approached Dad. His eyes—I will never forget them. They were empty, sad, distant. He was clearly trying to hold on, trying to function, but was barely able to speak or move. Dad motioned for me to sit down in a chair. I could hear a siren as the fire department arrived.

In moments like this I have now learned to be *present*, to simply *be with* the person in distress. On that day, though only an eight-year-old, I had no idea what to do, so I decided to simply be present. I learned this was a gift I could give to anyone. I could just hold someone's hand, offer them a tissue, hug them or sit with them as we all began to figure out what to do next. I learned it was okay to be silent, to not have all the answers.

Being *present* requires us to soak in who is there what is going on. As I have gotten older, I have also learned to say a quick prayer for God's protection. I used to take in the sadness, confusion and sense of loss, but it was exhausting. To be my best in these kinds of situations I needed to be quiet, be open and take everything in before saying a single word. Too often I see people who want to help say things that cause more harm than good. The worst of these statements may be "I'm sorry" or "I know how it feels". I have found that just *being there* is usually the best thing to do. Many times in these moments I hoped that I could be the hands and feet of our Heavenly Father: to show another human being love in action; to be kind; to give them hope that there is always love; to point to the love of God who never leaves us—ever.

On that day in the front room of a small house, I heard the mother scream, "Oh God, she's gone." My dad walked over to the father and mother and hugged them both. Dad softly said, "She is with God now. She is free from her earthly suffering. God has her now."

My daddy was a big man, six-foot-one and about three hundred pounds with a huge barrel chest. He was literally holding up the grieving parents as they began to fall into the grief of having lost their beautiful daughter to accidental suicide.

My dad fired at me his 'do not to cry' look from across the room. He had taught me not to cry in front of grieving families. It was our job to hold things together so that the family members could cry. Our time for grieving and crying would come later.

The truth is I cry for every single member of the church or community that experiences pain, loss and heartbreak. I cry giant-sized tears, sometimes so many that I'm sure I have no more left. I feel the loss of these dear ones and know they are crawling through deep, dark valleys. I know the grueling journey of grief that awaits them. I know that their lives will be forever changed. I also know that they don't crawl through those valleys alone because God's love and light is there giving glimmers of hope to hold onto. I told my dad countless times that I could never be a minister because I would cry all the time because of the sadness that comes through our lives.

Dad always told me that I could be anything I put my heart and mind to. He said that God had a plan for me and my job was to figure out what that plan was and then to be obedient to God. Many times he reminded me of the amazing growth and miracles that were rooted in deep loss. My dad said that we, as human beings, cannot know what a mountaintop experience is without walking through a valley.

I agree with my dad's wisdom, but sometimes I feel like it is just too much. I hope to have a conversation with our Heavenly Father about a few cases where people just fell apart and never recovered from their losses. It is the faces of these unrecovered people that I see, their forever-broken hearts are the ones that I mourn. Oh, how I wrestle with the losses that are just too much to bear. People can break—too much exclusion, too much hurt, too much pain. Our world tends to thrive on scapegoating. We all point to the other person, the one who is broken, without owning our own darkness and brokenness. What our world thirsts for is compassion and kindness as modeled by the one who was sent by God, his son Jesus Christ, who was fully man and fully God.

In the front room of that small house Dad went into action. He called on other members of the church to help this family navigate the next few hours, days and weeks. This was one of the most amazing parts of living in a small town. We always came together to help. Everyone played a role from planning the memorial service, to preparing the meal for the lunch after the service, to protecting the family's house while they were away. Everyone in our church played a role in helping families who needed support to move forward.

My father used to call on church members who had experienced similar loss or grief to help those in current need of support. On that long-ago day, Dad called on another family who had lost a child to suicide to provide help to the family who had just experienced such a heartbreak. Dad called these occasions *full circle moments*. He told me it helped both families—those serving and those being served. Both were healed in their loss and grief.

Dad reminded me that we still needed to head to church for the morning services, but we waited until other helpers arrived before we left.

What struck me that morning was the tragic loss of a teenager who hadn't meant to take her life, but did. I was astonished at the finality of death for this teenage child. I suddenly saw how caught up in life we can become, how blinded we can be by emotional pain and sorrows, and how we can lose everything.

You can lose it all because of the choices you make, so choose well. That is the lesson I gleaned that day. *Heather, choose well.*

Nothing prepares us for incredible loss, but I can tell you that even as a youth I had an incredible appreciation for how broken and painful life can be, even for a beautiful teenage child who seemed to have it all.

Getting Ready

In my youth, one of my favorite things was to walk through the church early Sunday morning before services. The church would be quiet and still. Dad would turn on the lights in the sanctuary and you could feel the holiness and sacredness present. I would run around the altar and jump on the box in the pulpit where Dad would stand and preach. I would mumble something funny, pretending that I was preaching or saying something important.

Dad would make his rounds and finally say, "Come on now, we have to get ready for service."

We would make sure that the paraments were in place, check that the hymnal numbers in the program were correct, and that the candles were fully stocked. Most of the time we remembered to do all of this, but on more than one occasion Dad would throw me the stink eye during service as several candles fizzled out. Oops! I immediately knew we had missed that step.

What was really fun was preparing for communion. I will never forget one hilarious service. At the time, I did not understand why the church folks laughed so hard, but looking back I now understand the humor.

One Sunday morning Dad said, "Heather, we'd better get to church early today. Gus is responsible for setting up communion, and you know he always forgets. Let's hurry up and check it out."

So we arrived fifteen minutes before the service and, as predicted, the sanctuary was dark and the altar was empty. No communion trays were out. Good old Gus had dropped the ball. Nothing was ready.

Dad turned to me and said, "Okay, I have to go pray with the Sunday school and choir now. My dear, it is up to you to prepare the elements for communion. The supplies are in the communion closet. Send someone to the corner store to get grape juice and bread."

All right, I thought, how hard can this be, even for a nine-year-old?

I confidently headed to the communion closet. I had played hide-and-seek in there for years so I knew the shelves, the beautiful silver trays and mini communion glass cups. I removed the communion linens and the silver cup and plate. I was off to a strong start.

I headed back to the closet. No juice there. So I raced to the Sunday school closet and got some fruit juice, thinking it was close enough. I located an adult and asked him to run to the corner store and pick up some white bread for communion.

I was flying along until I got the communion cup trays out and realized Dad had only given me half the story. I wondered what went in the inner ring of cups used by the adults. They were always a different color liquid and separate from the cups used by children and youth so they must contain something else, I concluded. Of course, at the age of nine I had no idea what wine was, where I could find it, or how it was supposed to look or smell.

I headed back to the closet and climbed up the shelves to a place where our former maintenance man used to hide his afternoon libation. Sure enough, way up there, all the way back in the corner of the shelf, was a dusty bottle. I brought it down, opened it up and took a big whiff. Oh yeah, it was stinky! It was perfect. I was sure that adults liked stinky things so this must be what went in the center cups. It seemed clear at the time that this must be what went into the glasses in the middle.

But there was only a little bit of the foul-smelling liquid left, so I added some water to make sure there was enough for all the adults. And I filled my dad's glass with it too, so when he led the congregation in communion he also had the elements.

Oh yes, communion was prepared.

The service started. Way in the back of the church were the Back Pew Boys. This was a row of conservative business owners whom I adored sitting with and chatting politics and business. It was with them that Dad put me when I was at church by myself. Needless to say, that strategy backfired on Dad because I grew up to be a fiscal conservative and my bleeding-heart liberal father was crushed. He often said it was his cross to bear that I voted for Ronald Reagan! Ha!

Mom was sitting in the pew next to me, so I told her about my very important mission to set up communion. She looked concerned. I told her, "No worries, Mom. I have it covered."

She asked what I had used for the elements and I told her. A tear started running down her cheek.

I ask her what was wrong.

She said, "Nothing is wrong, Heather."

I realized then that she was laughing. I asked why she said to be quiet and sit still.

As Dad lifted the chalice to his lips for communion you could see the look on his face as he smelled the contents of the cup. He immediately knew something was wrong but it was too late to fix. He glared at me from the pulpit. Again, small tears rolled down Mom's face as she desperately tried to hold in the laughter.

Dad began to distribute the communion trays. Mom and I both realized that the concoction I had made looked just like apple juice, and sure enough everyone grabbed it. Both young and old grabbed the cups in the middle of the communion trays. As they were being passed, you could hear the choking sounds of adults as the trays made their way through the church all the way back to the Back Pew Boys.

The Boys in the back pew congratulated me on my Sunday morning shots and quickly asked when I would be preparing communion again. They loved it. Needless to say, Dad wasn't impressed. I caught an earful after church.

Oh what a morning. Fortunately, the congregation soon saw the humor in my mistake and started laughing. I did feel compelled to share this story with the recruitment committee when I was asked to be a Junior Deacon. I asked if they would trust me to prepare communion and they said, "We bet you will never make that mistake again!"

Listen and Trust

It never failed. Any major holiday was when things really heated up at church. Because I was chair of the Emergency Committee and it was the Fourth of July weekend, something was bound to happen. It always did. That was the way it seemed to work. My father, the senior pastor, was out of town. The moderator of session was out of town. Who was left in town? Me.

My dad phoned early Saturday morning and asked if I could head over to the county hospital. One of our members had suffered a major heart attack and the family had asked for a visit.

As I headed to the ICU, I worked to calm my nerves and prepare myself for whatever I was walking into. Making hospital calls, I have learned, is like walking into an emotional vortex. Everything seems to be supercharged. A family in distress amplifies all the emotional energy that lies beneath the surface and you never know how that will play out. All the past hurts and stuffed emotions seem to flood to the surface—the good, the bad and the ugly. We all are broken, and you just never knew what to expect except the unexpected!

I stood outside the door to the ICU and said a prayer asking for God to help me find the words to bring comfort to this family. I asked Him to work through me to be whatever this family needed this morning. Needless to say, I was shocked when I saw dear Joyce on the hospital bed.

Joyce and her husband were wonderful members of our church. I always remember them as the family that planted Christmas trees. They even planted a beautiful Christmas tree in our front yard. It was so fun over the years to watch this tree grow.

Joyce's husband had passed away when I was young. I was always impressed at her grace and ability to survive the shocking loss of her husband. She was an amazing, vibrant and healthy woman. This stood in stark contrast to her state this morning. She was ashen gray and hooked up to many tubes. Her dear mother, who spoke broken English, held her hand.

I immediately joined the family around her bed. I listened and learned that Joyce's condition was very grave. The physicians and nurses were trying to convince the family that Joyce would not recover and it would be best to end life support. I tried to help convey this message to the family, but Joyce's mother kept saying, "It's not her time, it's just not her time."

I was with the family for well over an hour. We prayed together, talked together, and I tried my best to help the family come to the reality that was before them. Joyce was gravely ill and not expected to live. The hospital staff was trying to get an answer from the family to continue or discontinue life support. Joyce's mom kept saying, "It's not her time."

I could clearly see that the family was not ready to make any major decisions. I asked the medical team if the family could postpone a decision until tomorrow. Joyce's mom asked if we could gather around her and offer up a prayer for God's guidance and strength in making this decision. Boy did I feel pressure! At that moment I felt so inadequate. I was a twenty-something college kid offering up prayers on behalf of a cherished church member, and I had been trying to convince the family that perhaps it was Joyce's time to go. We prayed together, but as I offered up the prayer I thought about the grief this poor family would go through should they decide to end life support. I dreaded what tomorrow would look like.

I finished the prayer and left for home.

Early the next morning, I arrived at the ICU. A nurse greeted me and said, "You will never believe it. Go over and see for yourself."

I went into Joyce's room and she was sitting up in bed, smiling and holding her mother's hand.

Joyce's mom looked me right in the eye and said, "See, it wasn't her time yet."

What a humbling moment that was for me. How sure I had been that the medical team was right. I had been working with the family to end life support for Joyce. Now, sitting in front of me, Joyce was full of life. I had offered up a prayer the day before on behalf of the family but I had let my need to influence their decision get in the way of what was God's will for Joyce.

I learned an incredible lesson that day.

Joyce's mother had taught me about faithfulness. She had taught me that in our darkest moments we need to fully surrender to a power much larger than us. We need to enter into prayer not with a list of what we are expecting or what we need, but rather saying to God *your will be done*. We need to be faithful to God's will and God's vision of what we are to be. It is not up to us to have all the answers, but it is up to us to trust in God's will and know He will provide for us in difficult moments.

When we are called into holy and sacred moments, we need to release our need for control and be entirely open to God's hand. For as much as we think we are in control, there is a power and presence far greater than ours guiding us. Our call is to let go of our willfulness and submit to that power and to trust God's amazing grace and will for each of us.

There are Two Ways to Be Light

They say that it takes a spark to ignite a flame. There is also a saying that there are two ways to be the light of God. One way is to be the flame. The other is to be a mirror and reflect the light. These thoughts prompt me to reflect on my experience with someone who was a spark to my faith—a *reluctant* spark.

One autumn day my friend Maryanne called to share that she had been diagnosed with brain cancer. It was a very aggressive type of cancer and her prognosis was less than a year to live. I was devastated. I soon realized that her tumor was in the area of the brain responsible for speech. With a master's degree in neuroscience and some experience in hospital ministry, I knew that she would soon lose her ability to communicate.

During my first visit with her, we just sat and cried. At the end of our visit, I asked if Maryanne would like me to pray with her. She said yes. It was during our prayer that I felt Maryanne's body relax. She seemed comforted in prayer. I felt a holy presence and saw for myself how God had led me to be with Maryanne at that very moment.

In shock at the news, many of Maryanne's friends seemed to be unsure how to approach her and her family. My instinct and first reaction was 'to do' and spearhead the building of a support network that her family would soon need. As her needs became better defined, friends soon began to support this family.

Soon after our visit I learned that neither Maryanne's spouse nor the woman whom she had appointed to coordinate her caregiving were people of faith. While I believe both of these individuals were spiritual, they were resistant to any attempts to bring faith or religion into the house. I also discovered that my friend had closed the door on her faith, a door that had been active before her marriage.

What a spark this was for me! Never before had I entered into a space so resistant to faith. I wrestled with how I could best approach and support this family during its difficult time now that faith had been removed from my toolbox. At the time this felt like too much. I was being pushed into a place where I had to find my voice and a way to point to God. Oh, the long nights and countless tears. Looking back, I am so grateful for this opportunity—but in the moment it was tough!

At my next visit to Maryanne's home, I could see the cancer was progressing. I remember being very nervous on this visit as it was clear that any attempts to pray with my friend would be regarded as hostile. But God provided yet another spark. When I arrived at Maryanne's house I discovered her out-of-town parents were there and her husband and caregiving friend were not. As our visit ended I asked my friend if she wanted to pray with me. Surprisingly she nodded yes, she would welcome that. I noticed that her parents, who were in the kitchen, had stopped talking and were peeking around the corner. I asked them if they wanted to join us.

During this prayer her parents wept when I asked that God be present in this house as the family walked through this valley together. Her parents were active in their faith and had been experiencing enormous sadness because they feared their daughter was no longer active in her faith. They were afraid that "she was bound to a dark place." The gift of God was in her heart and this was so welcoming to them. We all wept as we prayed together.

Over our next visits, as communication with my friend became more difficult, I wrestled with the question of whether my friend was truly seeking God's presence or if I was imposing my faith and beliefs on her and her family. I grew more anxious each time I approached her house for a visit. What would I say if someone questioned me? Did my friend understand when I asked her if she wanted to pray? Maybe I shouldn't pray with her at all. I didn't want to cause any disunity in the house—my presence was intended to be one of comfort and love.

As time passed, the cancer rapidly progressed and my friend's speech became unintelligible. Before I paid another visit I called a friend who was pastor at Mt. Calvary. I asked him for guidance because I felt God was calling me to assure my friend of God's love and life everlasting for those who seek Him. Should I visit her? Should I pray with her? Should I ask her for permission even if she couldn't answer?

The pastor's resounding answer was to be fully present with my friend and rely on the Holy Spirit to guide me.

During my next visit I learned that my friend could no longer communicate. I kept trying to make sense of her words but they were just sounds bunched together. Nothing made any sense. Oh, the frustration in her eyes as she tried to make her thoughts clear to me. We decided that day to just sit together and hold hands. She laid her head on my lap and I rubbed her back. I remembered thinking to myself, *No more words, my dear friend.*

As our visit drew to a close, I asked her if she would like to pray for God's comfort and peace. She sat up, looked me straight in the eye with great clarity nodded yes. As I began to ask for God's presence, my friend began to mumble *God, God, God* repeatedly. I began to tear up, and just held her close, asking God to be with her, to comfort her and give her His peace. During our entire visit, my friend had not been able to produce any coherent words—not one word. But as we entered prayer, she began to call out God's name. God was with her in our prayer and He was with us in this moment.

At that incredible moment I realized that God had put me exactly where I was supposed to be. My friend had been a spark to me as I had been a spark to her. I was the light in the darkness of her cancer and she reflected that light back to me in prayer when we called upon God to be near to us. I was drawn closer to God through her illness, her loss of words, and then the miraculous gift of her calling His name. After my reluctance, the gift of being God's instrument was one of the most amazing and humbling miracles I have ever experienced.

There was another spark for me in this experience—that of becoming more keenly aware and sensitive to the world around me that does not know the story of God's good news. By being entirely open to where God wanted me to be, I was able to be of service in a way far greater than I ever had before. I have heard it takes courage to enter into someone's suffering. What truly takes courage is being open to where the Holy Spirit leads you, and to not fear the destination but know that God will provide for you once you are there. As the saying goes, there are two ways to be the light—one to be the flame, the other to reflect someone else's light.

I challenge you to be open when God calls you to be the light, and when he calls upon you to reflect the light of others.

Fancy Pants

I will never forget the afternoon that we heard my dad bust through the door laughing so hard that he could not speak. His face was red and tears were streaming down his face. We knew that he had just been at a graveside service, and so we could not for the life of us figure out what had happened and why he was laughing so hard.

Having and keeping a sense of humor is critical in ministry. With all the heartbreak you experience, you must hold onto blessings. I've held onto this one, and through it all it's one of the funniest stories I can recall about my dad and being a preacher's kid.

It happened on a Saturday afternoon during a wet spring. The melting winter snow had turned almost everything into a muddy mess. For the families whose loved ones had passed away during the winter there was always a rush for a graveside funeral as soon as the ground had thawed.

I seem to recall that we were sitting in the kitchen when my dad came through the door. His face was bright red and he was laughing so hard he literally couldn't breathe. All we heard were squeaks and what we thought was deep laughter. We couldn't tell if he was choking, crying or laughing. We waited as he made his way to the kitchen, flailing his arms and struggling to get his words out one by one. First he said "Tent". Then he said "Shoes". He made a plopping sound and then said "High class man from New York City". We did not know what to make of it. This is what we eventually learned about his graveside service.

Dad said he had received a call from a fellow in New York City, a funeral director who seemed to be very unhappy about having to travel from New York City to Western New York for the burial of his client. As the local pastor, Dad agreed to preside at the burial. When he arrived at the cemetery he saw the usual tent, gathering of family members, casket and open gravesite.

It had been a miserable morning with mud everywhere. Most of the local folks from town had worn their puddle boots, but as Dad shared, the fancy funeral director had on his very expensive dress shoes. *Oh boy*, Dad thought, *this could be interesting*. You see, working a graveside funeral is tricky business, especially on a wet and muddy day. Lots of things need to happen. The funeral director needs to be very smooth, so as not to upset the family, and to keep things dignified and respectful for the dearly departed.

As my dad was presiding over the ceremony, he observed a guest standing in the corner of the tent. She was half under the tent, half outside. This guest seemed to be using the leg of the tent to pull something. Dad couldn't see exactly what was happening, but something was up. He also noticed the tough time the New York City (NYC) funeral director seemed to be having maneuvering under the tent to facilitate the burial. He was slipping and sliding all over the place. As he got ready to lower the casket, my dad was concerned about his ability to stay on his feet. But the casket was slowly and smoothly lowered into the ground.

Dad breathed a sigh of relief and asked everyone to bow their heads in prayer.

As everyone bowed, my dad glanced at the woman holding onto the tent pole. On closer inspection he saw that one of the woman's fabulously expensive high heel shoes was stuck in the mud. She was using the tent pole as leverage to get her high heel unstuck, and this time she was putting all her body into it.

As Dad began to say the prayer, the funeral director was standing directly in front of the open grave in which the casket now rested. The woman by the pole had lost her balance and swung around the tent pole, her bare, panty-hosed foot missing its fancy shoe still stuck in the mud. Her foot came flying around the pole and straight for the NYC funeral director's backside, connecting with his two-thousand-dollar suit and kicking him straight toward the gravesite.

Dad desperately tried to continue praying and remain dignified for the family. But he told us that you could hear the slipping sounds of the funeral director's shoes as he danced around the graveside opening, trying not to fall in, and finally coming to rest at the edge of the hole. He was quite disgusted and full of mud. Dad had held it together, finished the prayer and was counting the minutes till he could get into his car.

Dad said the funniest part of the story was watching the woman hobble away from the funeral with one high heel shoe on and the other muddy shoe in her hand. He said he would never forget how she kept her composure and gracefully hobbled away as if nothing out of the ordinary had happened.

After the family had left the gravesite, the NYC funeral director cursed his way back to his car saying he could not wait to get out of this God forsaken town. For all the antics, the family was able to lay its loved one to rest and did not seem to notice the flying bare foot or the scampering funeral director.

Dad was able to keep it together until he got to his car, at which time he said he has never laughed so hard in all his life. To keep the laughter inside was one of the hardest things he has ever done. I tell you, life as a minister is never dull, and God has a fabulous sense of humor. The key is to be respectful, show grace under pressure, and be able to blow off steam when you return home. And never get so tired or stressed out that you can't laugh. Life can be hard. Ensuring that you have the capacity to manage what the day brings is critical, especially in the ministry.

I Am Not Prepared

A church is almost like a living being. It has a certain pattern, rhythm or flow. There are times where many weeks will pass and life will be quite normal, almost mundane. Then, without warning, the church family will experience several illnesses, deaths or emergency situations.

Growing up, I was always involved in one way or another at the church. My father was the senior pastor and I enjoyed the opportunity to minister by his side. He would take me from hospital beds to family rooms and inner city soup kitchens as easily as going to soccer practice or flute lessons. Oddly enough, I loved it.

I am not sure if it was the fact that I got to hang out with Dad or if it was the excitement of what we would encounter. Needless to say, I took it all in—I didn't want to miss a single moment of my dad ministering to those in need. I was always astounded by his ability to always say just the right thing at the right time. Whether praying with someone before surgery, helping a family saying goodbye to a loved one or after services on Sunday morning, he always nailed it.

When I was in college, I was given the opportunity to serve as a deacon in my church. A deacon literally means to 'shepherd' the members of the church. Our job was to provide care for members of the congregation as requested. Responsibilities included hospitality and ministering to the ill and lonely to name a few. The board included several leadership positions and I chose to head up the emergency committee. I liked this committee because you never really knew exactly what the needs were going to be or how you would be called upon to answer that need. More often than not it involved a hospital visit or helping someone grieve due to the sudden loss of a family member.

My dad came to rely on my abilities as a church deacon. Without fail, anytime he was out of town, usually for continuing seminary studies, something would happen at church that required his attention. But at a time of limited cell phones, no internet, or the inability to communicate on demand, the church would turn to me.

There is one occasion in particular while I was in college and my family was on vacation. I remember getting a call from the church secretary sharing that a member of the congregation and one of my dad's very dear friends was not doing well. Charlie was in the veteran's hospital and his condition was very serious. Once I received this news, I called my dad to see if he knew any additional information; he didn't, but he encouraged me to contact the senior church leaders so that they might be able to visit Charlie. As fate would have it, everyone was out of town. I would have to be the one.

I called my dad to explain the circumstances, and as we spoke I could feel my dad's sadness as he realized he wouldn't be there to say goodbye, to hold his old friend's hand, or to offer him comfort through prayer in his final moments. Charlie was more than just my dad's friend; he was also a mentor and close ally.

Charlie was the executive director of a homeless soup kitchen in downtown Buffalo, New York. He had been an advocate for the homeless for many years. My dad and Charlie worked together for years to raise awareness about the issue of homelessness. Our family had come to love Charlie for his dedication and ministry to homeless men, women and children. As you can imagine, for all of us, learning that Charlie was nearing the end of his life was difficult news to receive.

I realized that this visitation was truly up to me. I needed to represent our family and our church, pray with Charlie, and lift him up in his final moments. I felt totally unprepared for this moment. Although I was not formally trained as a lay leader, I had spent years with my dad helping provide this kind of support. Even with this experience, I told Dad that I just couldn't do it this time. I didn't know what to say, I didn't know what to do, I wasn't prepared for seeing an old friend through his final earthly moments.

"Dad," I said, "you always know exactly what to say. You always get it right."

I will never forget my dad's comforting words. "Heather, it isn't about me. I am simply God's instrument. There are times when I don't say anything at all. It is simply about being fully present with those who God would have me be with at that moment. Everything I say, everything I do, comes from a higher power. *You* can do this—*you* can be God's instrument too."

I hung up the phone with a new dose of courage and confidently left for my visit with Charlie. Once I arrived at the veteran's hospital, though, I entered rather reluctantly. As I began to search for Charlie's room through the labyrinth of corridors, I was overcome by the nauseating stench of urine and the unforgettable hospital odor I remembered as a child from visits to sick relatives. *This certainly was not the happiest place to be*, I thought as the elevator slowly moved up to Charlie's floor.

I was scared.

It is an amazing thing to see someone who is close to death. The body changes dramatically, most noticeably in the loss of weight, the change in color, and the transparency of the skin. It always shocks me. Reluctantly I entered the room. Charlie was semi-conscious in bed, struggling for each breath, still wearing his trademark bottle-thick glasses. Tubes were everywhere, machines were beeping, chiming and lighting up the room like Christmas. This was the real deal. Charlie was not going to be part of our world much longer.

Charlie had no family that we knew of. His family was the church and his ministry was his passion. I knew that with the church elders and my family being out of town for the weekend, I was the only face that Charlie might recognize. I gathered myself, took a deep breath, sat on the side of the bed and took Charlie's hand in mine. I leaned in close and told him that I was here on behalf of my dad. I told him how much we loved him and how much we admired his spirit and his ability to give voice to the voiceless. I explained that Dad was out of town and not able to be here today. As I spoke, my eyes were transfixed on Charlie's hands resting in mine. When I finally looked into Charlie's semi-open eyes I could see a tear-streaming down. Even though he was not fully conscious, it was clear that he understood what I was saying.

With a renewed sense of courage, I asked Charlie to pray with me. As I called for God's presence, I asked for his love to surround Charlie. I called on God to comfort him and provide him peace. I prayed that Charlie would soon come to know God's full comfort and love. I gave thanks for all that Charlie had been and all those who Charlie had loved and cared for. Even though Charlie had strayed as a young person and done horrible wrongs, he had made changes in his life and dedicated himself to serving the most vulnerable. For the years after he served time in jail, Charlie had been a good and faithful servant. He had loved and cared for the unlovable—those who we pretend not to see on the streets; those we are afraid of; those who have no place to go. Charlie had been the true deacon for the homeless. For most of his adult life he had offered them hospitality and fellowship. He loved to 'be' with those who were on the edge of our society. He used to have his pension checks sent directly to the soup kitchen. Through terrible loss and being broken, he had awakened and found a calling that he attempted to fulfill every day of his life.

I thought about all the lives that he had touched, all the people that he had helped, all the service that he had provided without asking for anything in return. And now he was just a shell of who he once was, clinging to this world even as he longed for the next.

I wanted Charlie to know he was not alone, that he was loved and cared for and it was okay to drop his earthly limitations and run into the outstretched arms of our Savior so he would be free from pain.

I ended our prayer and kissed his soft, wrinkly cheek. I rose from the edge of the bed and looked at him and said, "See you later, Charlie," and then turned and left the room.

I made my way to the elevator, this time oblivious to all of the smells and sounds that had been so bothersome when I arrived. The elevator took me back down to the lobby. As I left the elevator and began to walk towards the exit, a nurse called to me. Clearly out of breath, she had been trying to catch up to me. Grabbing my shoulder, she told me that just after I walked out of Charlie's room he had passed away.

Just like that.

Charlie had taken that final step and was now with his Maker.

I stood in stunned silence trying to make sense out of what had just happened. Dear Charlie had been holding on these last few hours for something, someone, perhaps a sign that it was his time to go—that his time on earth was done and his mission was accomplished.

I felt so privileged to have been able to be there to lift up Charlie to the Lord and share our love for him before he passed. I had been given such a blessed gift. And now I more fully knew what Dad meant about simply being God's instrument. God had prepared me by giving me the courage through my faith to find the words that would allow me to be his instrument.

This was never about me. It was about God working through me to minister to someone who had cared for so many of his children. In the end, Charlie was dwelling with God. That is the desired end for each of us—to be with the One who created us. Amen!

True Hospitality

October 1995—I can remember it like it was yesterday. I was on my way home from another stressful day of work as special assistant to the U.S. Attorney in Buffalo, New York. I was listening to the radio and feeling good because that evening I had nothing planned except to go home and crash on my couch. Or so I thought.

I've heard that if you want to make God laugh you should tell him your plans.

It was the top of the hour and the day's headlines were hitting the airwaves. I was only half paying attention to what was being said as I contemplated a relaxing evening at home. But suddenly I heard the words "Highway 400", "East Aurora" and "armed and dangerous". Everything in my brain stopped. My heart began to race because my family lived just behind Highway 400 in East Aurora. Whatever this breaking news was, it was happening in my family's backyard!

The reporter stated that two armed and dangerous men had recently escaped from a prison transportation bus in that area. Most of the other fugitives had been caught, but these two had escaped. Officials were very clear that everyone in the area should close and lock all their doors and windows, turn off the lights, and by all means remain indoors until these fugitives had been apprehended. My stomach began to knot up. I realized that something big and dangerous lay ahead of me, something unknown and frightening.

Let me give you some background before moving on. My dad, a pastor, began his ministry in the 60s in Washington D.C. during the height of the civil rights movement. By his own admission he was a bleeding heart liberal. He held dearly his responsibility to offer hospitality to all, especially the marginalized, the excluded and those on the edges of our society. He came to life when he preached that our calling in life was to be beacons of hope in a dark world... to be where Jesus would be, on the side of the powerless, the broken, the sick, the vulnerable, the lost, the forsaken. That was where Jesus was. And as a twenty-something, I was totally unprepared, totally unequipped for what was about to happen, but shucks, I was my father's daughter and I had been living these kinds of adventures for years. Surely I was overreacting... my gut must have been misfiring. Maybe it would be nothing.

Still, part of me wanted to head back home and hide my head under my pillow. But I couldn't. I was going to have to be in this—whatever this was.

As I listened to the radio reports, I just knew my dad was at home opening every door, turning on every light and probably out looking for the fugitives. He wanted his house to be the beacon of light for everyone. I knew that in Dad's mind these men were simply innocent victims of a "broken" criminal justice system.

Making this situation even more dangerous, Aurora was and is a very conservative town. I feared this news flash would give permission to everyone in town to grab hunting gear to help protect the town. Soon pickup trucks and rifles would abound. Furthermore, my co-workers at the Department of Justice were some of the very people seeking to get these two fugitives back in custody. Great!

This was going to be a fun evening. Oh boy!

Visions of a relaxing evening quickly vanished as I turned my car around and headed into town. I picked up my cell and began dialing my family to find out what was going on. No one at the house was answering. They were ignoring me. I just *knew* the fugitives were in the house. My gut was telling me that somehow Dad had coaxed these "armed and dangerous" fugitives into our house with my mom and brothers. I kept thinking, *He has no idea what he is doing.*

Selfishly, I was thinking, How am I going to explain this to my work friends. Oh yeah, that guy who welcomed and hid fugitives in his home? He's my dad. Great. This will be fun. Not!

Fearing the worst, I called the church legal counsel where my dad had been pastor for many years. My hunch was the family was harboring the fugitives somewhere within the church. I wanted to know how much trouble my dad and the church would be in when the fugitives were caught... not to mention transporting a fugitive. I could just see my dad driving these fellows in our family van down Main Street, probably hiding them under blankets. Good grief. Could a church offer sanctuary? Intuitively I knew that my dad would find or had already found these young men and would offer them sanctuary.

The attorneys offered their assistance but said we should call the police. They were concerned for everyone's safety. And they were not alone.

I once again tried calling home. This time my teenage brother answered. It sounded like pure chaos in the background as I asked what was going on.

"What do you think?" my brother shot back. "You should have seen our home. Every other house in the neighborhood is pitch black, but not ours. All the doors are wide open. All the lights are on. Our back yard looks like a landing strip and our house looks like a lighthouse with a sign reading *All On-the-Run Convicts Welcome Here!*"

My dad had actually been out looking for the fugitives and found one hiding in a tree in our back yard. Of all the trees in town, this guy had to pick one of ours to hide in! Dad was actually in the kitchen feeding this criminal dinner and dressing him in warm clothing. My poor brother said, "Heather, this guy is wearing my favorite sweatshirt. It's crazy."

My brother then shared that they were going to transport this guy to the church because, of course, Dad had offered him sanctuary.

Oh great, now my dad's list of crimes was growing to include transporting a fugitive.

I yelled at my brother to call the police.

In a calm and steady voice, my brother said, "Heather, he's only a kid. His name is Miguel and he speaks no English. He is seventeen years old and is so skinny he was able to slip his hand out of the handcuffs. He's scared and we need to help him."

Oh great, I thought, now Dad would have company in his jail cell—my brothers were now accessories.

In the background I heard Dad yelling to my brothers to get into the van. I wishfully asked my brother if they were taking Miguel to the police station. "No." They were going to the church, and I should meet them there in Dad's office.

Well, I thought, isn't that nice and convenient. Dad's church is directly across the street from the police station.

I was almost into town by now and driving as quickly as possible without drawing attention from the police or the potential vigilantes that may have been out there. I pulled into the parking lot at church, and as I walked in I found my brother standing guard. I asked him where Dad and Miguel were hiding. He looked me over and demanded my cell phone. "Seriously?" I asked.

"Seriously," he answered.

I surrendered my cell phone and my brother motioned for me to follow him. We walked into the dark church and straight into my dad's office.

"Where's Dad?" I asked.

"Stay here," my brother responded. I found out later that while I was in Dad's office, my youngest brother and Dad were off hiding Miguel in the bowels of the church.

As I looked out the window I saw a constant stream of police officers and concerned citizens looking for the bad guys. Oh, how I feared the police were going to storm the church!

While I sat in Dad's office I bowed my head. "Dear God why here, why now?" As I prayed it became clear to me how Dad could be a part of this but what about me? I didn't sign up for this. This wasn't how I wished to be active in my faith—this wasn't on my list. I had other plans.

My prayers were interrupted when my dad entered his office. I kept trying to think about how I could keep him safe. That was one of the biggest challenges with Dad, he never gave a thought to his safety. He spent numerous nights ministering to the homeless in dangerous places and would never give his safety a second thought. He knew that he was serving His God and doing the Lord's work. He went where he was called—no questions asked. He had a deep belief that where he was called, God would protect and provide. His trust took him places that I think even law enforcement would say, "No thank you."

I told Dad that I was scared for our safety. I worried that the police would storm the church.

He told me that they would never do that.

I quickly replied, "You wanna bet?" I asked him to share what he knew and what his plan was.

My dad said, "Miguel needs our help."

"Can I see him?" I asked.

"No way!" Dad answered. "You'll turn him in."

I told Dad that my number one concern was for the safety of our family, and that I didn't care about some kid from Nicaragua who broke the law.

Dad spun around and looked me square in the eyes. "Heather Lynne—you just don't get it, do you?

This is God's house and we are called to minister to the sick, the lonely, and those in jail. We are called to offer hospitality to all. God put us here for a reason."

As the words left his mouth and began to saturate my head and heart, I stood completely still. It was convincing. I called myself a person who followed Jesus Christ. I loved the verse he was quoting, Matthew 25 about our call to be with the lonely, sick, broken and excluded. And here I was trying my best to get this fugitive back to law enforcement.

This was one of the big ah-ha moments for me. Was I going to live out my faith? Was I going to do what the Bible so clearly asked in scripture?

As my head was swirling with thoughts, I tried to pull together a plan where we could keep everyone safe and still get this young man, whoever he was, to safety. And keep my dad, my brothers and my church safe.

After convincing Dad that I was there to help and not to turn in Miguel, Dad finally allowed me to meet the fugitive. This was one of those moments that will stick with me forever. I was scared. My heart was pounding through my chest. I was about to meet the fugitive that everyone said was armed and dangerous. Dad called for my brother to bring Miguel into the room.

I stood there motionless as a skinny, small boy entered the room. His head was hung low and he was quivering with fear. Intuitively, I sensed his innocence.

This young man did need our help.

"Okay," I said to Dad. "What's your plan?"

Dad rather sheepishly said, "I have no clue. That's why you're here."

I now knew why I had turned the car around and come to East Aurora instead of going home to a quiet evening on the couch. Once again, my dad needed my help to get through a sticky situation! I told everyone in the room that if we were clueless, then we needed to rely on a higher power to help us through this sticky situation. And we needed to get started right that instant.

Even though we were all scared we wanted so desperately to help. We also felt helpless. We joined hands and surrounded Miguel. We called for God's presence and wisdom. Soon, calm entered the room. Things got quieter—the chaos lifted. After our prayer we were able to think more clearly and soon our plan emerged. While I was still afraid of the police storming the church, I felt like we did have a story to tell and that we could be the beacon of hope that would help Miguel navigate this storm.

I had taken several years of Spanish in school but had not used it for some time and was quite rusty. Even so, I was able to get some useful information from Miguel. He had come to the United States in an attempt to find members of his distant family. He had been arrested and was now due to be deported. He feared he would be murdered upon his return for fleeing the militia. So this kid did have a story to tell and we might actually have grounds to keep him in the U.S.

I soon realized that we needed help with language and legal advice. I placed a call to a top defense attorney and in no short order he said we were crazy and that we should turn over the fugitive. Needless to say my dad didn't like that answer so we went with plan B. Try to understand Miguel's side of the story. As I feared for our safety I thought if we had media covering this the police would be less likely to storm a scared place. I called my friend at the local CBS affiliate and asked him to send a team to my dad's church ASAP.

As soon as the media arrived I sent my dad outside to place a call for help—we needed someone fluent in Spanish so we could better understand Miguel's side of the story. Within minutes of Dad's call for help a woman arrived and she was ushered into my dad's office. With her assistance we were able to learn Miguel was from Managua and was just a teenager. As a child, he and his twin brother had been recruited by the Nicaraguan militia. During this time, his twin brother had been murdered. Miguel, fearing for his own life, had fled to the United States and was arrested as an illegal alien. He was in custody awaiting deportation. He was not armed and definitely not dangerous. He spoke no English and was scared for his life.

Knowing the full story, my dad granted him sanctuary and we pledged that we would do everything in our power to help him. I called the United States Attorney's office and explained our situation. They assured me that they would do everything in his power to ensure that Miguel would not be deported to his country. Okay, we were making progress.

The calls I made to my contacts in the media paid off as we were able to ensure that the local media would be on site to cover the transfer of Miguel over to the authorities. I figured that as long as there was media attention at the church, this would ensure that the police would not storm it.

With the media cameras on the church property and the guarantees from the U.S. Attorney's office were relayed to the police, we were ready to transfer Miguel. Before we did this, we gathered in my dad's office, joined hands and lifted Miguel up in prayer. The shear panic had left him and all of us. We were comfortable and confident that he would be treated fairly and that he would not be deported.

As we walked Miguel out of the church doors, we literally surrounded him with our bodies. We walked him across the street to the police station while the police had guns drawn on us. Although terrified, I knew that we were not walking alone. I could feel God's presence among us. We made it to the police station and delivered Miguel to the authorities unharmed.

Eventually Miguel found his relatives and came to live in the U.S.

I learned a lot that evening from my dad. I came to more fully understand that God calls us to be a part of His plan in His time. He calls on everyday people like you and me to help. You don't need to be wealthy, famous or highly skilled to be part of His plan.

I also came to more fully appreciate how every one of us can be a beacon of God's light. We need to be open to where and when God calls us... even those places that we don't want to go... even those places that you cannot for your life figure out why God would send you there. Everyone can be God's instrument as God guides us and flows through our lives.

That evening in 1995 was a good lesson for me. I am now more open to trusting God, like my dad was. I witnessed how God had surrounded each and every one of us. He is everywhere. He is present, and He is so good.

As we strive to grow in our faith and be more disciplined, I would challenge each and every one of you to look for the face of God in others. Be the light in the darkness. Be courageous and be more trusting in Him. Offer hospitality and look for Him. He is there and He is waiting for you to be the face of God to others. Amen.

Sharing Love with Her Last Breath

One of the greatest gifts my great aunt gave to me was showing me and my family how beautiful it can be when someone passes away. So many times death can be traumatic. It can be stunning and absolutely devastating. But death can also be this amazing opportunity to embrace your loved ones and come to peace with your time in this world as you head into the next. This was the gift that my great aunt June gave to those she loved.

June's health had been failing over the years. Her kidneys had failed and her life was now about dialysis. She was not one to sit still so the hours in the dialysis clinic were beyond painful for her. She had a wonderful life and all of these complications were taking a toll on her—she was ready to say goodbye.

As we gathered around her bedside, we of course tried to talk her out of this decision. We adored this woman who was born a century before her time. But she was a teacher and we were soon to be pupils in her final lesson. She was going to teach us about saying goodbye.

We knew that as soon as she stopped dialysis she would have about a week to ten days until her body would fail. We gathered around her bed, we prayed together, we told stories of her amazing follies; we truly were fully present with her. A moment that I fondly remember was as we were singing hymns. The look on her face, the joy of being surrounded by loved ones, knowing that you are being sent off from this world on the wings of love was such a moment.

As the week passed and June's body began to shut down, she slipped into a coma. Her nurses were just incredible. I even remember them singing to her. Such love surrounded her. June's time in this world was short.

I remember being at breakfast with my dad at the hotel. As he was enjoying his breakfast, I remember feeling so uneasy. I said to my dad, "There is no time to eat, we have to go." For on more than one occasion my intuition had been spot on. He dropped his fork and said, "Let's go." We raced to the nursing home.

We entered June's room. Her breathing was very slow and labored. We held her hands which were so warm. We told her we loved her; we told her it was okay to go; we told her she was not alone. We were here with her sending her off. The next part for me was beyond incredible.

The time in between her breathing widened. I looked at Dad and he looked at me and then we both looked at June. She worked to take a labored breath and then nothing. We sat by the bed waiting for another breath. Silence. Nothing happened. A couple more seconds past... still nothing. More silence. I said, "Dad, I think she's gone." I put my head to her mouth to see if I could feel or hear her breath. Then her mouth opened and with her final breath she whispered, "I loooove youuuu..." Then complete silence. No movement, no nothing. That was it.

I was stunned. I did not move. I did not breathe. I just stood there in that holy and sacred moment. I turned to Dad to ask him what we should do. Should we get someone? What happens next I asked? He said, "Let's just be here. Let's sit with her for a moment." We sat for a couple minutes.

I said I needed fresh air and almost ran outside. I just started walking, half aware of my own body, half numb and spinning. I looked around. It was amazing. Life just keeps on going. Not even death stops the world, not even for a second. It just keeps on moving forward.

I looked up to the sky. What happened next was surreal for me. In the sky there was this amazingly beautiful puffy cloud. I could see a brilliant sun behind the cloud, almost bursting around and then bursting through the cloud. This sun beam burst through the cloud and shined right down on me and the nursing home. As I felt the warm sun on my face, I could feel this amazing burst of wind and energy go right through my body and lift upward. I knew that my dear Aunt June was on her way to the next place. Her last gift to me was this amazing gift of love, peace and grace. For in her last words she had blessed me with her greatest gift, an affirmation of her love for me, truly the greatest gift one can give and share with another.

I have shared this story with individuals and families learning how to say goodbye. Finding the beauty in saying goodbye and fully trusting our Heavenly Father in the process of saying goodbye is very powerful.

I encourage you, the next time you are in a place that is scary or unknown to call God into that moment and trust Him. And I mean fully trust Him. Our Heavenly Father always provides what we need, when we need it. The vision He has for our life is far more incredible than we as individuals could ever imagine.

Psalm 46 (ESV)
Be still and know that I am...

No Coincidences in Christ

I believe we have the opportunity to see God in our everyday life if we are sensitive and willing to see Him. The things that happen to us often are truly miracles, but too often we choose to overlook them. In our rush or wanting to stay safe and not engage with strangers we miss opportunities to learn more about ourselves and to be connected to other human beings. The following story is an example of what I call "no coincidences in Christ".

During a frigid February day in Minneapolis, when my son Jacob was just two months old, I had the opportunity to fly home to Buffalo to visit my family and friends. I wanted my friends and family to meet our latest addition. This trip was also planned so I could also have the chance to say goodbye to two dear friends of mine—a church member from my dad's church whom I used to visit frequently as she became house-bound and my best friend's father, who was terminal with cancer.

Like any mother flying with an infant, I was anxious as I boarded the plane. Jacob had never flown before and my mind raced with concerns not only for him, but also for my fellow passengers. Would my son cry the whole time? Would he disrupt the other passengers? Would the air pressure bother his tender ears?

As Jacob and I climbed into our bulkhead seats, I turned to a friendly-looking gentleman who was seated next to us. I apologized in advance for whatever disturbance Jacob might cause. With a huge smile on his face, the man quickly shared that he was happy to be next to a newborn. I felt very lucky to be seated next to someone who was kid friendly for the flight.

The gentleman had noticed my name written on my ticket and asked if I was related the former Senator of Minnesota.

I said, "Yes, in fact Jacob is his grandson."

At this point the man introduced himself as Stan. He was a career government employee and in the past had testified before one of my father-in-law's committees in the Senate. What a delight to learn this. Stan's face glowed as he talked about the days when he had served our country.

I began my preparations for the flight. As I was digging into my oversized purse/diaper bag, it became clear that I was having trouble managing everything. Stan noticed I needed help and asked what he could do.

I sized him up and asked if he could hold Jacob for a moment so I could get organized.

He whole-heartedly accepted the invitation. As I handed over Jacob, Stan's entire face lit up and his eyes began to fill with tears. *Wow!* I thought. *This guy really loves babies.*

As Stan held Jacob, he began to share the heartbreaking story of how he had just recently lost his only son to appendicitis. I told him how sorry I was for his loss and how pleased I was that my dear Jacob could keep him company on the flight. I felt like we were put next to Stan for a reason.

We arrived in Buffalo and I thanked Stan for his companionship and care of Jacob. I felt good about meeting Stan and perhaps playing a small part in his life. Even with an infant, I had been able to connect with a stranger and make his day a little brighter.

That weekend was very special as I was able to have my family and friends meet Jacob for the first time and say goodbye to my former church member and friend. I was also able to spend time with my best friend and say goodbye to her father with prostate cancer. It was a weekend filled with feelings and meaning on so many levels. Everywhere I went I shared the story of meeting Stan—of his kindness, his loss and grief, and how little Jacob was able to lift his spirits.

As the weekend drew to a close I found myself with Jacob back at the airport. After tear-filled farewells to my family, I walked down the jetway to board the plane. As I scanned the lobby outside our gate for a convenient place to sit, my eye caught a familiar face—my new friend Stan! Jacob and I went over and sat next to him. After a hug and exchange of the usual pleasantries, we compared seating assignments and, sure enough, our seats were right next to each other again. This certainly was no coincidence!

I asked Stan if he was a person of faith. When I don't get this right the first time, God has a way of telling me that I missed something. Stan said he was a man of faith and so we immediately began to compare notes trying to figure out why God had chosen to bring us together, again.

As he shared the details of his weekend, I learned that not only was he in the same hospital at nearly the same time as I was, but he was just two doors down on the same floor visiting his mother. We had missed each other by minutes.

When I heard this, tears filled my eyes. Another amazing coincidence! Or was it?

I handed little Jacob over to Stan and both of their faces lit up. Jacob snuggled into Stan's arms. I was still amazed to see how a newborn baby could bring such peace to another human being.

During the flight Stan shared more about how he had lost his son to appendicitis. Everyone had missed the telltale signs—fever and back ache. His son had waited too long to seek medical attention. How devastating it was! And how Stan must have hoped that others would not wait to seek medical attention.

I listened intently to everything he said trying to discover what God was trying to accomplish through us.

Upon my return home I told everyone the story of Stan and our coincidental encounters. I told my family in western New York, my fellow volunteers at the Junior League, and all my friends. I felt compelled to share the incredible story of how little Jacob was able to touch the life of this stranger who had now become a friend.

After telling this story many times, I came to the conclusion that the purpose of meeting Stan was to help him cope with his immense grief. Jacob and I had been placed in Stan's path to help him. It must have been that—or was it?

What happened over the course of the next several weeks was a true miracle. Within weeks of my return to Minneapolis, both my brother and one of my Junior League colleagues developed backaches and high fevers. They had remembered the story I had shared about Stan's son and the missed symptoms. As a result, they both immediately sought medical help and both were diagnosed with appendicitis. Their successful surgeries may have saved their lives. Praise God.

There was the true meaning of the 'coincidental connection' with a fellow passenger on an airplane. It was certainly no coincidence that I was seated next to Stan not once but twice. It was no coincidence that Stan and I had visited loved ones in the same hospital only two rooms and a couple minutes apart. It was no coincidence that my brother and friend both had appendicitis attacks within weeks of my meeting Stan.

Clearly, this was God's way of providing a message of love, healing and the Holy Spirit through a "coincidental encounter". How truly amazing this was. The tapestry of our lives and the people who are put in our paths are interwoven on a daily basis.

God is truly at work in our daily lives. When we take the time to slow down and make meaningful connections with other human beings we can see His Glory and Grace revealed to us. This experience affirmed for me that there are no coincidences in Christ. You only need to be open to seeing them. So my question for you is—what might you see today? Look around. Your next gift or miracle could be nearby at this very moment.

We're Gonna Make Our Connection

I was in Appleton, Wisconsin, for a one-day business trip. I knew I was pushing my luck as it was my daughter's birthday. I told her, "No worries—Mommy will be home for your birthday dinner." I was confident my flight would give me plenty of time to get home for dinner, cake and presents.

My meetings wrapped up right on time and I caught a cab to the airport with time to spare. The monitors all reported the flight was on time. *No worries.* I sat down at the gate and waited to board the plane.

The closer we got to boarding time, the more airline staff began reporting to our gate. More and more maintenance workers began appearing and quietly heading into the plane. Not a good sign, I told myself, but there was no official word of a delay. The gate area was packed, and with time ticking by everyone was curious about why we had not yet begun to board.

As I continued to see more maintenance workers file onto our plane, I turned to the very polished executive next to me and said, "This is not a good sign."

He quickly agreed.

Within minutes, a boarding agent reported over the loudspeaker that the plane was having technical issues and we would need to be rescheduled on other flights.

I turned to the gentleman next to me again and said, "Oh no, I'm going to be in trouble with my daughter. It's her birthday."

He shared that he needed to make a connection so he could say goodbye to his mother on the west coast who was on her deathbed.

What a shift in perspective I experienced!

I turned to the man and said, "Tell me more."

The gentleman told me about the heavy burdens he was carrying including his mother's illness. He was the CEO of two international corporations and both his heart and body were weary. I listened and asked questions. As he was talking, I began to silently pray for him. All we could do was wait.

As others began to book other flights I sat there trusting that we could make this connection, and that this gentleman would get to see his mother by late evening. I kept praying and asking how I could support him here and now.

Eventually I noticed the boarding agents return to the desk. They announced that parts had been located and the flight, while delayed, would in fact be returning to the Twin Cities.

A cheer resonated throughout the gate area. I turned to my new friend and told him how pleased I was that he would soon be on his way to the West Coast.

Slowly we were called to board the plane. As we were walking to the jetway I could feel my heart beating so strongly I thought it was going to leap out of my chest. During the time we had been waiting I had not shared my faith but I didn't want to impose on my new friend. As we were in line together I touched his shoulder.

He turned to me and I boldly said, "I don't know if you are a person of faith, but I am. And right now it is on my heart that I should give you the book I'm reading."

I had picked up a copy of Ruth Haley Barton's book, *Strengthening Your Soul for Leadership*. This book is phenomenal in helping readers open their eyes to the realities in their choices, the importance of self-care, and the importance of being connected to our living God. The book had really challenged me to think about my overdoing, over-committing habits. In the name of faith, I had become a human *doing* rather than a human *being*. I was exhausted and didn't have enough energy left to serve my family, let alone others. It was clear that I had to change some habits and make time to be with God.

That was my main takeaway. It's not just about going to God with a check list of needs. God created us so we could dwell with Him—that we might sit with Him and listen to the Holy Spirit's call. For many years I had missed this point and I had committed to shifting some things inside me to be better connected to God.

My friend said he was of faith too. He happily took the book, and we entered the plane and parted ways. As an executive frequent flier, he quickly moved to the front of the plane and I proceeded to the very back.

I took my aisle seat and was able to see him grab the book and begin to read. My heart leaped—he was *reading the book*. In fact, he read it for the entire flight. I wondered what would happen when the flight was over. Would he run away? Would I see him? Would he wait for me? Would he have questions? Would he feel better? Might this help him in some small way?

When we exited the plane he was waiting in the gate area. He had the book in his hand. I asked him what he thought about it. He said the message was exactly what he needed today. Running two major multimillion-dollar international organizations was taking its toll on him. He had worked with an executive coach in the past, but that was mostly about head smarts, not heart and soul smarts.

I asked him if he had finished the book, but he hadn't. I told him to keep it because I felt he would find more value in it today than I would.

He asked if I had a connection in Minneapolis and I told him I was home and was happy to talk with him as he walked to his next gate.

Here is the most awesome part of the story. Several weeks later I received a beautiful note from him thanking me for our time together. He had finished the book on the second leg of his journey and it had caused him to do some self-reflection, just as it had with me. He shared his gratitude for my being there for him. Then he shared a book by a leadership guru who his firm had brought in. He really encouraged me to write down some of my own stories so I could share them with others.

What a gift for me to hear back from someone I had interacted with. I see it as an affirmation to keep going and keep pointing others to invite God into the tricky situations of life. When you are out and about—in a grocery store, coffee house, the sidelines of a game or in the workplace—if your heart begins to pound and you have the feeling that you are about to connect with someone, take a deep breath and trust that what you need will be provided. And then go for it!

Breathtaking Loss

My father passed away unexpectedly, and as that reality penetrated my body I could literally feel the air empty from my lungs. I collapsed to my knees on the floor. I had lost one whom I loved dearly. I shouted to God, "Please don't take him. Not yet. I am not ready for him to go." As I lay on the floor, I closed my eyes and said to myself, *breathe—you are not alone, breathe. You can get through this with God's help. Just keep breathing. Breathe...*

I tried to picture in my mind the glory that Dad was experiencing. I tried to imagine daddy seeing our Heavenly Father face to face. In that moment in heaven, God and Christ Jesus did not seem so far away from me because now someone who was so dear to me was there. Heaven seemed more real to me. Closer. Possible.

As I began to walk the path of grief, I found that worshiping in church was tough. Because so many of the memories of my dad involved church and hymns, I could not sing anything anywhere after he passed. It literally hurt when I heard hymns being sung. This couldn't continue. I needed to get back to church. I needed to be able to be worship.

I decided I needed a plan if I was ever going to be able to go to church again. So I bought a couple CDs with hymns and I played them as I drove. The first few times I cried so hard I literally had to pull over. My kids thought I was crazy as momma cried every time she got in the van and turned on the radio. But slowly it got easier. There was one song, *It's Not Far From Here to Jesus*, that was the hardest one for me to hear, let alone sing. It took a solid year to overcome the emotional effects of hearing and singing hymns, but thanks to God's grace I was slowly able to get through parts of the songs, and eventually entire songs.

As the years have gone by, I have come to know that God is not far from any of us. His love and grace surrounds us even when we are not deserving of his precious, unconditional love. For our Heavenly Father tells us in Romans 8:37-39, that not even the powers of hell nor powers in the sky above or in the earth below will separate us from his love. We are God's children. We are his beloved.

God also shares in Deuteronomy that he will run across the heavens to our aid when we call on Him.

Imagine our creator racing across heaven and earth to answer the call of one of His creation. Our God loves each of us and showers His love and compassion on us.

C.S. Lewis wrote that while God whispers to us when life is good, he screams to us when life is full of heartache and struggle. God is with us—in fact, within each of us. He's not far from us even when we turn away from Him. God awaits our return.

When you are sad, when you are sick, when you are lonely, when you are in jail... if you suffer from an addiction, a broken relationship, or a living hell... please know, please remember as *Newsong* shares in their song: "it's not far from here to Jesus. His loving arms are open wide."

The Business Card

Dad's passing, while not completely out of the range of possibility, was completely unexpected for me and it shook my world. He had been in poor health and developed into a fragile diabetic. At sixty-four he had given everything he had, including his health, to his ministry as a pastor. The concept of sustaining your soul for leadership was one that was absent from our household. Within hours of his passing we flew from our home in Minnesota to his apartment in Florida. Dad had slipped away. Now what?

I was still healing emotionally from a miscarriage when we learned that I was pregnant again. This was just days before I heard that my Dad had passed away. I never got to tell him the news that we were given another chance at having a baby. Still fresh from the miscarriage, I was terrified that I would lose this one. I kept telling myself to keep it together. I became very protective of the new life inside of me.

But how was I going to protect that new life while saying goodbye to my dad? His passing was heart-breaking and terrifying. How could I do this?

Arriving at his apartment was eerie. Everything was just exactly as he had left it. His cane was by the door, his shoes lined up ready to be worn. Everything was waiting for him. We slowly entered this quiet and lonely place and began to get ready for the work of packing up his life.

I went into my dad's office seeking important paperwork. My brother and husband went into the dining room, and my other brother went into the kitchen. It was a small apartment so we talked out loud as we stumbled across different items. I stood in Dad's library—mostly in shock—scanning the room with all its the memories.

This was just too incredible. Where do we begin this task ahead of us and how do I care for this little life inside of me?

How do I do this, God?

Suddenly I heard my brother call me. "Heather come here. You won't believe this. You just won't believe it."

My brother had found my dad's Bible on the dining room table. Dad had always worked at the dining room table. He liked to spread out his papers on the table and be in the middle of all the action. I can recall many a spat between my parents as Mom

93

had wanted to get dinner on and Dad's papers were piled high. Being in the thick of it was where Dad worked best.

This was where my brother went to see what Dad was working on right before he passed away. We wanted to know more. We wanted to have some sense of where he was. What was he thinking, feeling and doing? So many unanswered questions.

As we gathered in the dining room, my brother Paul pointed to Dad's Bible. He opened it up and showed us something that was marking a page. What section of God's Word was my dad reading? Why was it marked? What might we glean from Dad's last time in God's Word?

While we were all spinning in grief, here before us was a treasure far beyond anything else we had found that week. Inside the Bible was a bookmark. The bookmark Dad used was my business card and it marked a page in the Book of Matthew. The verse Matthew 25:25 was highlighted.

Now we were all sitting at the table and my brother Paul and husband David came to show me what they had discovered in the verses. Matthew 25 is about the importance of using your talents to minister to those who are lonely, hungry, sick and imprisoned. It highlights the importance of using our talents and encourages us to make the most of them.

Wow! In the process of healing from the loss of a pregnancy, I had been wrestling with the question of what I should be doing with my life. It is amazing how a loss or injury can really send shock waves into your world. Loss gives you fresh eyes and a damning filter that you didn't have before. What seemed important or worth investing time and energy in just doesn't cut it anymore. Be it friendships or volunteering, everything now was shifting inside of me. With the loss of my dad, I could only imagine the big questions that would be emerging in me.

Through this internal conversation, I had been struggling with how to work differently. How could I add value in the world? What should I be doing? What were my gifts and how was I uniquely made and formed?

Here in my valley of grief came an answer. My father had been reading scripture. And he had been thinking of me. This was a gift to help me transform how I worked. I needed to shift my work from direct service and trying to do everything on my own (hmmm, fiercely independent—yup that fit me) to mentoring leaders. This shift of doing *for* others versus doing *with* others was a major insight. By working as a catalyst and coach, I could multiply the impact. This new discernment challenged me to think about what my strengths were and how I could use them to help others unlock their potential.

A second and perhaps even more profound insight from this scripture was that God for centuries had been calling upon his people to use their gifts to do the work. He had been calling upon us to serve the lonely, the broken, the imprisoned and the sick, often in places that were not easy to be or culturally popular. Time and again we are called in God's word to be His hands and feet.

This scripture was like a beautiful road sign— Heather, you need to get off the highway and turn here. You need to use those gifts that God has given you and you need to help others see me and use their God given gifts to help others.

In one of my deepest moments of sorrow, I had been given a gift. Over the next year I often found little signs from the universe that I was supposed to be helping others dive into the question of who they were... how they were gifted and how they might use the gifts that they had been given to do something beautiful. Only God can take such pain and turn it into good. He can make such things happen and I give Him praise and glory for how He can work all things for his good. Amen.

Deeply Rooted

On a day about ten years ago I had four hours to pack my family for a journey to my father's memorial service in New York. Coming off a week in Florida as my dad's executor and managing his estate, I was scattered, tired, and pretty much a wreck. I literally didn't have the energy to care about anything. My close friend Cathy had been checking up on me since Dad had passed and called before I had to catch the flight. I told her how I was feeling and she invited me over. I warned her of my state of mind, and she said, "Come over. My mother happens to be in town and I think she can help you."

At this point, I thought, Well, honestly, what do I have to lose?

When I arrived, her mother greeted me at the door and gently put her arm around my shoulders and led me into a small room. She sat me down and then asked me to remove my shoes. She said,

"Sink into the chair and let your feet sit firmly on the floor."

Okay, I thought. *I can do this. Now I just need to relax.* I must have looked like a two-by-four in that chair—exhausted, stiff and completely stressed out—honestly, a big hot mess. And six weeks pregnant. Yup, morning sickness and mom of two children under the age of three-and-a-half. All out of sorts and totally not relaxed.

I closed my eyes and tried to take a deep breath that made it as far as my throat. Here we go.

Cathy had told me about her mother's gifts on a couple of occasions. Her mother was trained in the ministry of healing prayer. She had ministered to the sick and was able to help others understand where they were in those broken moments and helped invite God into their hurt. Today I was a perfect candidate for her gifts. I was completely open to the fact that I needed something far beyond what this earth had to offer. At this point, if she was offering to help, I was game.

Her mother lit a candle and said something under her breath. I understood that she was inviting a higher power to join us that morning. Heaven knows I needed it. She began by asking me to envision roots growing out of the bottom of my feet and going deep into the earth. Deeper and deeper. I imagined my roots diving into the earth like a grand tree. I envisioned these roots firmly holding and connecting me to the Earth. I began to feel something I could hold onto. I was no longer drifting helplessly in this ocean of grief and being swallowed whole. Something was slowly shifting. I was beginning to feel connected and grounded. Slowly, I felt my feet again, and then my legs. I was gaining back enough strength to stand.

Cathy's mother then asked me to envision the air in my lungs, reminding me that air was all around me—all around the earth. As I was filling my chest with air, I was doing the same as those who had come before me, and those who will come after me. For the first time in a long time I was connecting to my breathing. I was visualizing the air filling my lungs. Until this point I hadn't realized that for most of my life I had been disconnected from life, from breathing. *Wow, this is what it feels like to really breathe and be connected to my breathing.*

I recalled that beautiful scripture in Genesis about God breathing life into the dirt and making human beings. I could feel my feet firmly rooted in the earth, and now I could feel life filling my lungs. Slowly, more strength filled my soul. I was coming back to life. Stress was peeling away—I could feel it leaving my body and life replacing the stress and pain.

Then Cathy's mom moved to my heart. "Can you feel your heart beating?" she asked. "Can you feel the love and health that is in your heart, Heather?"

Yes, I could.

I continued to connect with my breathing. Suddenly I recalled all the sympathies that friends had been showering on me. I connected with the love that I felt in my heart and all around me. Little did I know that all this love would begin to form a shield of protection that I could lean on during the months ahead of me.

Even though a love had been lost, other love was there. Love had always been there but I had been moving so fast as a young grieving mother that I literally had lost touch with it. I hadn't been able to fully see or feel it. But here and now, through this simple exercise, I was reminded. I knew I was reconnecting with the inner love and peace that surpasses all understanding. Cathy's mom was guiding me and pointing me to God's love and light. She was guiding the light throughout my being to heal me, to help me return from a deep dark place.

As she continued to guide me through the exercise I became more and more relaxed. I felt more grounded. I felt stronger. I could literally feel a healing power surround me and within me. Never before had I allowed myself to be still, to breathe and to experience such a level of peace and understanding.

Following that prayer, I had a strength, clarity and resolution that I have never experienced before.

To be in such a peace-filled place was immensely powerful. It was life changing and transforming, another gift that had come from immense loss. Cathy and her mom had helped me gather and re-center myself, reviving a sense of love that I could stand firmly upon as I continued down my grieving path.

I was now able to collect myself and my young family for the travel to Dad's memorial service. I am a pretty efficient person, but when I returned home and literally had ninety minutes to pack two children and two adults for our trip, I did it with unexpected ease. My sense of well-being not only sustained our travel, but I carried it to the lectern. As I prepared to give my dad's eulogy, I felt strong—fully present and calm. I shudder to say this, but I actually enjoyed being able to share how great my Dad was and how much I was going to miss him.

This shift from utter despair to hopefulness was truly amazing. I felt a level of peace that surpassed my understanding. To this day I hold that peace in my heart, knowing that when we call upon God to sustain us, He does. He keeps his promises and what a transformation this was for me. My hope is that from my experience others can discover the value and gift of reflection, of healing prayer, of God's amazing ability to heal and carrying this into your life. I invite you to try it and see what happens.

Ashes to Ashes

The day finally arrived when I was to honor and bury my dad. All I needed to do was deliver his eulogy, host a celebration reception, and spread his ashes in the memorial garden at the church. I kept telling myself, *Heather, you can do this.* I tried to keep focused on the tasks at hand, knowing that huge land mines lay ahead with the particular family dynamics that were in play. You see, when my Dad passed, my family's emotional baggage simply exploded. It was simply too much.

Let me explain one of those family dynamics. My dad's mom, my grandmother, literally hates my mother with all her being. They really *hate* each other! I love my Mom and my grandmother and had been able to tiptoe around this reality since being a little person. But with Dad's passing the gloves were off. My dear grandmother couldn't understand why I would invite my Mom to Florida to help me.

Mom and Dad had separated and divorced because they were better apart than they were together. While the decision was hard on both of them, it was just the way it was. Marriage was hard, being a parent was hard, and doing both of these while being a minister was even harder. I had come to peace with their divorce, but clearly my dad's family had not. His death meant this was going to be a highly-charged week.

I was six weeks pregnant, just off a miscarriage, responsible for managing Dad's estate, and raising two young kids under age three. I needed help. I knew while it would be hard on her, Mom would jump on a plane and come help me if I called. And she did. Of course, my grandmother was furious.

Great! I thought. Here we go. Just another day in paradise. Deep breath Heather. Lean into God and trust He will give you what you need. Trust Him, trust him deeply.

With the help of my husband David and my Mom we got our two young sons dressed and fed in time for the church service. My brother Paul and his family, and my other brother Todd, were all staying at Dad's place because we wanted to be close to what was left of my dad. In fact, at times we found ourselves waiting for him to come out of the bedroom to surprise us. Dad would have been so happy that we were all there! But of course we all knew he would not be coming.

That morning I was more nauseated than usual. At six weeks pregnant this was a good sign, but no one except my husband, my mom and my brothers knew this piece of information. I was terrified because I had miscarried a couple months earlier. *Keep it together, Heather* I kept telling myself. *Don't over-react. Don't do anything to lose this baby. Just hold on.*

Whenever I speak in public I get nervous. I can't eat and usually my face and neck flush until I begin speaking. I get butterflies and that morning was no different. *I can do this. Keep it together, Heather. Trust you will be sustained and provided for.*

At the church, my husband David got the boys situated in the nursery so I could find a quiet spot to prepare my remarks for the eulogy. In my mind I kept saying, *You can do this*. I wanted to nail this so badly. I wanted the whole world to stop for one minute so I could scream from the highest mountaintop how great my dad was. I wanted them to know how filled he was with the Holy Spirit, how his life pointed to One Who was greater than him and his humble ministry. I wanted them to know how he gave his all for ministry—how generous and compassionate he was. I felt an immense responsibility to share his story and plant seeds of hope and understanding in the hearts of those who would be with us today to celebrate his life.

My dad loved funeral services. He would tell me, "Heather this is my chance to reach those who don't know God or who don't have a church family. This is my chance when life, or in this case death, has caught their attention and we have a small moment to break through the busyness and the daily grind to say there is a God who loves you."

Even more important this day was my decision to be bold. I think that is the most surprising thing about death and grief. Boy, can you really become bold. In seconds you realize that life is short, so if something is important to you, then you'd better get to it.

As I had prayed about what to share about my dad's life, I decided I was going to broach a subject that I'd kept quiet about my entire life—how my dad was a wounded healer. This would be my first step in sharing this information publicly. He'd struggled with mental health issues my entire childhood. I hadn't planned to say this directly, but somehow I wanted to deliver a subtle yet clear message that he had been suicidal most of my childhood. And yet, in spite of his personal and emotional hurts, in spite of those challenges, my dad was an even better and more compassionate pastor because he quietly wrestled with his own demons every day.

With all of these family issues in play, I had yet another challenge. My grandmother had *demanded* that my mother be banned from the sanctuary during the service. It was like a storm that had layer upon layer of stress and many opportunities to fall apart. But through all of it I kept going back to a place of peace and boldness. I kept holding onto the promise that through this mess God was present, and through this ordeal God would guide my steps if I continued to trust His will.

I begged my mom, "Please hang in the back of the sanctuary out of sight. I want you to see the service, but it's Dad's mom who is making this demand. Please let her have this time and we will have another service in New York for our family to say goodbye as we want to."

God bless her—she honored my grandmother's request. But I knew that my grandmother would still find fault and let me hear about it. I was afraid that my grandmother and my dad's family would emotionally devastate me that week. This storm was brewing, but on the day of the memorial service I needed to focus on honoring and burying my father. After all these years of seeing families in grief, it's ironic that my dad's family would take the prize for dysfunction.

I toyed with the eulogy title *Peace in Heaven, Hell on Earth*. It surely fit the bill because that is where I was on that day, walking this path of land mines with the irony that this wasn't about me or my siblings. This was all about my parents, grandparents and aunts who were dysfunctional and the shadow that is cast on the next generation. The damage they caused to us kids was ridiculous and here I was trying to tip toe and keep everyone behaving—ugh!

I thought I had mapped out all the dynamics in play. I was now prepared to enter the sanctuary and get Dad's memorial service underway. I took a deep breath and began to walk the hallway towards the sanctuary when I saw the funeral director. He was carrying something.

Hmmm, I wondered what it was, Still, I continued down the hallway with the beautiful Florida sunshine streaming through the window. The funeral director walked toward me and now I could see he was holding a white cardboard box. His lips were moving but I couldn't hear any words. I was in a zone, mentally preparing the eulogy of a lifetime for my daddy.

What was the funeral director saying?

He motioned for me to stop. He was trying to get my attention. I stopped and he approached me, handing over the white box along with a clipboard and some paperwork and a pen. Obviously I needed to sign something. The paperwork said something about... *what*? Did it say *transfer of human remains*? As I had requested, there were two bags. He said that my grandmother wasn't happy about the dividing up of the remains.

I kept trying to figure out what he was handing me.

To this day I cannot understand why anyone would hand over the remains of a loved one in a cardboard box seconds before the memorial service. Never in my years of funerals have I encountered such a thing.

My focus started slipping away. My beautiful, peaceful zone started to disintegrate. Being prepared for the eulogy went out the church window.

Then it fully hit me. Oh my God, he was handing me Dad's ashes. The funeral director opened the box to show me that he had bagged my dad's remains in two bags as requested.

I looked at the bags. I saw ashes—just like the ones at the bottom of the countless fires we had started in our fireplace and campfire. My dearest Daddy was ashes. This was so deep for me. Dad wasn't here.

He was really, really dead. He was not here.

My mind flashed to all the Ash Wednesday services I had attended over the years. I could see my dad imposing the ashes on my forehead. All those times my dad had said to me, "Remember that dust you are, and to dust you shall return."

Oh my gosh, get me the hell out of this state, get me the hell out of this church, get me out of here. I wanted to throw off my shoes, grab my baby boys and run all the way back to Minnesota. That's it—

whatever capacity I had to manage, everything was gone. I was D-O-N-E!

What do I do? I thought. I have my dad's remains in two plastic bags and my note cards to deliver his eulogy.

I tried to get control of my thoughts. *Okay Heather. Keep it together.*

I closed my eyes and prayed. Dear God, this is crazy. This is too much. Help me to honor my dad. Help me to keep this baby. Dear Lord, I need you now.

Without even missing a beat, my husband David appeared and slipped his arm under mine. He literally caught me as I began to fall apart. He always has been my saving grace. He looked deeply into my eyes and brought me back from that dark place I was running to. He held my arm and smiled. He didn't try to fix anything. He didn't say a word. He just stood with me. He was God's hands and feet in that moment. My heaven-sent David stood by me and I knew that love would win this day; even when those we love do bad things, even when others are insensitive, even when the actions of others hurt deeply, God's greatest gift—the gift of love—always endures.

I can do this.

In a flash, I was back. Naturally I'm pissed off at the funeral director, but I don't want him to know that.

I gathered my thoughts. I can't carry this ugly white cardboard box into the sanctuary. No way—not for my daddy. What can I do?

I felt my Coach purse on my shoulder. Perfect, I love Coach, and Dad did too. It will have to do.

So I say to my dear husband, "Help me empty my purse so I can place Dad's remains inside."

I looked into my purse. Daddy, bet you never thought that it was possible for you to be inside a Coach bag. But into my purse you go. I gently placed his ashes into my purse.

I gathered my notecards, grabbed my husband's arm for dear life, and together we marched right into that sanctuary with the piper already playing the bagpipes. We walked to the front pew. I very carefully set my purse on the pew and then took a seat.

All those years of helping others deal with deep grief. All those times that I had walked with families into memorial services or hospital rooms or graveyards. Now it was my turn to walk the walk.

Yep, this was happening.

Those that attended the service said they couldn't believe how composed I was. They told me that I glowed as I talked about Dad and his ministry. They appreciated the messages of the wounded healer and the promises that God makes—including that *love never dies*.

That day I truly felt honored as we buried my dad. What a ride it had been. That day I was forced to learn to lean heavily on the promises of God and those that He places in your path to be His hands and feet. We are provided with exactly what we need, when we need it most.

Through all of it I simply hoped I would my do my part well for my daddy. whom I adored.

A Mourning Dove

About two weeks after my dad passed, my husband and I were sitting on the back porch when we heard the strangest sound. It sounded like a wounded bird getting closer and closer. We rose to our feet and began to look for the injured bird. It sounded like the bird really was having problems. From the side yard we saw a mourning dove that looked like it had never flown before attempting to land.

We stood in amazement as this mourning dove landed right in front of us on the deck, making the most God awful sound we had ever heard, like *Look out, here I come.* We managed to get quite close to the bird and stared in amazement. What the heck was this bird doing on our back deck?

Let me share some of the events leading up to this moment. Prior to losing my dad in June of 2004, we had lost a baby due to a miscarriage in April. My heart was still broken from losing that baby. I wasn't yet healed, and I cried every night into the little blanket they gave me at the hospital when they performed the D&C. So when my dad passed a couple months later, I was devastated. I literally felt like someone had pulled my heart and soul right out of my body. The loss was so tremendous, it literally hurt to breathe. I was sure there was no way I would ever laugh again, never enjoy anything again ever. I was toast. The only silver lining for me was the fact that the little one we had lost was now with my dad in heaven.

I remember the moment when my husband got off the phone and shared with me the news that my dad had passed away. I had crumbled to the floor screaming, "God, not now. I am not ready to do this on my own. Please don't take him away from me. He is my talking post, he is my compass, and he keeps me steady." What was I going to do without my dad?

I found that many of my friends were offering me prayers of peace. I was in such a fog I couldn't really remember many of the details of those first few months. My body was going through the motions, but my heart and soul were in limbo. I was pregnant again, had two young boys and a husband to care for, and so much of what I focused on was care giving for my young family. I kept telling myself, "Okay, I can make it through today. With the help of God and the prayers of my friends, I can do this. Just keep going."

Friends kept offering prayers of peace for me. It was interesting how my prayers were answered for me over the course of that first year. My call to God was an external one. I was seeking peace for the soul of my departed father. Although I was praying for peace for myself I was not ready to accept the gift of peace that God offers.

I began to pray for peace from my immense sadness and broken-heartedness. I prayed for peace over and over again. As the tears rolled down my cheeks every evening, the prayers would come for peace. *Would peace ever come? And what would peace mean for me?*

And then that one day a mourning dove kept arriving on my back deck. It came and sat for hours as the boys and I would play on the deck. We talked to this darn bird and asked it if it didn't have some other bird business to take care of someplace else. But this bird was determined to be a fixture on our porch. My boys greatly enjoyed visiting with the dove and came to seek it out whenever we were outside.

About a week after the bird starting visiting I had an ah-ha moment. I realized that I had been praying to God for peace every night. And here on my back porch was the animal that symbolizes peace—a *dove*.

As one who seeks meaning and purpose from the world around me, I began to contemplate what this meant. Okay, I thought, God sent me a dove. Was this to encourage peace? Was this to remind me that we never walk alone, that God always walks with us? What did it mean?

As summer passed, my family came to enjoy our visits from the dove. Sometimes it would appear at the most amazing times. For example...

On my oldest son David's first day of school, we were waiting at the bus stop and he was wearing the backpack that my dad had gotten him. At that moment I so wished I could call Dad and tell him about David's first day—about all he was missing, about all that was happening. As we were waiting for the bus, I looked up to take a breath and gather myself. Sure enough, on the telephone wires directly above the bus stop and David's head was that same darn mourning dove.

I said to David, "Hey, little guy, look up. Our dove is with us this morning."

I wish you could have seen the smile on David's face. It warmed both of our hearts to think that a higher power might be with us that morning to help us along our path to healing.

We had so many of these coincidences with the dove that I began to wonder about another level of meaning with this bird's presence. I went back to prayer and really pushed myself. When would God give me peace? When would this immense burden of loss and grief ever lighten? Would I ever laugh again? I kept praying for peace, inviting God into my loss and grief.

Please help me through this, I cannot do it alone.

Around the time of my birthday I had another ah-ha moment. I woke up early one morning and there was the dove on the back porch again. As I sat staring at this bird I reflected on how the final years of my dad's life had not been easy for me. On the day he died my prayer had been selfish. He was in pain, suffering as a fragile diabetic. Perhaps my dad had been praying to God for relief from his burdens and his pains. Maybe Dad was tired and asking for a very different prayer than the ones I was lifting up.

By stepping back and reflecting, I could begin to see that my Dad was free now from earthly matters and pains. He was dancing with angels and free from all suffering. He was at peace. Perhaps this dove was here to let me know that Dad was at peace.

I saw this as an answer to my prayers. My dad was released and free from suffering!

It took many more months of work on my part to be okay with this because I desperately missed my dad. But I knew that I had to step back from what I needed and be okay with what Dad needed and had asked from his God.

Going into the Christmas season, I felt like I had really made progress with the loss of my dad. The tears kept coming each night and I assumed that I would cry myself to sleep for the rest of my life, but that was just how it was going to be.

That was one long winter for me. My young boys kept me moving and the arrival of my daughter in January gave me new purpose. After all the losses in the previous year, God had blessed me with a daughter whom I named Hope to remind me of the hope that God gives each of us, even in immense loss and desperation.

When spring arrived I was amazed to see the return of that same mourning dove. I remember asking my husband, "What am I missing here? Why is that darn bird back?"

Each night I still prayed for healing. I was not yet whole—not fully healed. I still ached for a measure of peace. For several more months that darn bird just kept coming back to our deck. It wasn't until the anniversary of my dad's passing that I had yet one more ah-ha moment from my friend, the mourning dove.

I was on the porch talking to the bird. My neighbors must have thought I had flown the nest for sure. But here I was talking to this bird. "Why are you still here? I get it. Dad is at peace, go on to another family and help them along the way. I'm done. I get it."

As these words left my mouth, I realized I had *not* gotten it. Not at all. It wasn't that Dad was at peace. It was that *I was not yet at peace*. My mind, heart and soul were still healing and I had not released myself of all the sadness and grief. I was holding it with clenched fists and I wasn't letting it go. God had been offering me His peace and I had stubbornly been pushing it away for over a year.

As I had my ah-ha moment, that darn bird looked at me, cooed and flew off. His job was done. I had finally allowed God's peace to penetrate and begin to heal my broken heart and soul.

Through this journey, whenever a wall of sadness would come over me or I would feel overwhelmed, I learned to not *fight* the tide, but rather to *float* into it and ride the tide. I did not drown but instead learned to honor my grief and mourning.

Does the mourning dove come back and visit? You bet he does. He comes and reminds me that I do not walk alone. No one does. I know in my heart that God walks with me and gives me what I need, when I need it. But does this make the hard work of grief any easier? Hell no. Grief is exhausting work, but good work. For I have seen how it devastates those who deny it. Grief becomes part of your experience, but it does not define who you are.

Honor your grief and look to nature for God sightings, for we don't walk the valley of grief alone. We are in good hands if we are open to seeing it.

Learn to open your clenched fists and offer your hurts and burdens to One who can truly heal you.

Wishing you God's peace.

Emergency Crosses

One of the downsides to being the minister in a small town is that everyone knows where you live. When life hits the fan, and you need your pastor, and no one answers at the church, you just go to his house. Be it domestic dispute, full mental breakdown, death in the family, loved ones facing addiction, a financial crisis—we as the pastor's family never knew what was on the other side of the door.

We would often try to tell those who arrived at our door that our dad was out. But regardless of what we would say, the person knocking always needed something. They would offer to wait on the front porch till he got home. On one particular occasion a woman with a history of mental illness arrived. She was in a schizophrenic crisis. "People" were out to get her and she wasn't going anywhere without something, anything from Dad. Everyone who appeared at our door knew they would be heard, be seen, and be given a small dose of hope. No judgement, no blaming, no lectures—just love and hope to get them to the next step, whatever that was. That was what my dad offered so freely and beautifully. He could meet you where you stood and love you through it.

No matter what a person's economic class, race, preferences, habits or personal demons, Dad welcomed in everyone and offered God's love and light. Boy, how I admired that as a kid. To meet anyone where they were and offer them a safe space to be during a rough patch... that is what I marinated in as a child.

What is so interesting for me looking back is all those years of community leaders and CEO's, and the so-called powerful, and the so-called weak—I saw them all for who they were in their broken moments. Standing at our door I saw those who beat their kids and wives, those who couldn't stop their addictions, those who couldn't love themselves... or others. As a little person I saw what was behind the masks, and it was a transforming experience.

So as people came knocking, we told Dad in no uncertain terms that we needed something to give them so they would know we were sharing their needs with Dad. Prompted by this "demand" by his family members, Dad reached out to a woodworker in the church and they came up with a brilliant solution.

Emergency crosses.

I still have a jar of them today in my office. I keep one in my car, although I painted it baby doll pink so it is my style. I have my emergency cross at the ready for whenever I need it!

The design was simple. Made of wood, it was three inches tall by two inches wide. We kept the crosses in a jar by the front door. We would offer them to whoever showed up and needed one. We would say a brief prayer, take information about their needs, and then they would go on their way. Of course, if they were stoned or drunk we had them sit in the front hallway till they came around.

This reminds me of a story. My mom loved to garden. One year she worked (I should say we *all* worked) to help build a beautiful new flower bed right in the middle of our front yard. She was so proud of her garden. In our area, it wasn't unusual for us to get two or three feet of snow, and that had happened this particular morning.

The doorbell rang and I ran to answer it. There at the door was a well-respected surgeon in our community whose four-by-four had slid through the snow right up the middle of the yard and directly through my mom's new flower bed. I couldn't believe it! Part of me wanted to laugh out loud. The other part knew my mom would be devastated. *Who drives through a flowerbed? Clearly, someone who isn't thinking straight.*

That was when I turned without missing a beat and said, "Dad, it's for you."

We used those emergency crosses everywhere. I took them with me to hospital calls, Dad took them on pastoral calls. We always had a huge stock of them. Dad even kept them in his car. Even in retirement, when Dad would walk the beaches to minister to the homeless, he had a stash of crosses. He shared many stories about executives who would travel to Florida for work conferences and end up talking to him for hours on the beach. Dad said that although he was retired his ministry was as active as when he was the head of a church. The emergency crosses were sure handy to have.

When my dad passed away and I went to the funeral home for the viewing, I ran out to his car, which we were using for errands, and pulled out one of his emergency crosses from the front cup holder. In my heart I wanted Dad to have one of his precious emergency crosses with him in his eternal rest. I asked my husband David to give the cross to the funeral director to place with my dad's remains. Just knowing that Dad would have an emergency cross gave me such a wonderful feeling. To this day, I carry an emergency cross with me just like the one I gave to my dad. It is a very powerful connection for me between the living and the dead. It serves as a daily reminder of how precious life is.

Yep, right up to the end, Daddy, your emergency crosses always saved the day!

Growing up, I saw poverty, brokenness and all kinds of misery come to our front door. Where do I begin to share all I have seen and witnessed from my front porch? How do I share what I have seen? How do I share that each of us carries burdens, each of us is broken? How can I share that no matter your wealth, your power, your status, your title, we all do things that separate us from God's love? And no matter how far we wander, God places people in our lives who can help point us to one that is bigger than ourselves and loves us unconditionally.

I'll tell you this much—I have emergency crosses in the car. I never leave home without them because I need my cross just as much today as I did when I was a kid answering our front door.

Finding Joy in Breaking Down at Joe's Auto Parts

Have you ever been happy when your car broke down? Well, I have to say I never thought I would, but I was actually thrilled when I broke down this winter. You see our family vehicle is an eleven-year-old van that has served us well. Our plan was to replace the vehicle in July, a mere five months away. While I hoped we would make it, the clicks, screeching fan belts and jerking of the vehicle did leave me doubtful.

Because we live in Minnesota, I placed warm gloves, boots and hats in the trunk in case of a break down. With a stretch of minus-thirty-degree days, I was really worried about it. Then one day, the weather—or I should say *winter*—broke. It was thirty degrees and the sun was shining. I was driving home along the freeway when the van suddenly hesitated and I thought, *oh dear, this is it.*

Dear God, I prayed, *help me to be safe.* A sinking feeling came over me. I tried to fight it but I have to tell you I wasn't so sure what would happen next.

As I was trying to figure out what to do I speed dialed my husband. No luck. I left him a message. Who else could I call? My mom. Again no luck, so I left her a message asking for her to cover me in prayer to help me get home safely.

Somehow, I managed to make it to the off ramp and was able to coast to an intersection. The light stayed green and I continued to coast. Off the highway and now on the main drag, I looked to see where I could park the car and call for help. All the time I just kept praying *please help me God... guide me.* Do I turn on this street? No, one more—turn here. I turned and slowly the van came to rest. I tried the accelerator and nothing. The van was done.

I lifted my head to check the surroundings. Low and behold I had come to rest right in front of an auto parts store. I finally was able to reach my husband. As we talked about next steps we both concluded that maybe we were meant to fix the vehicle rather than replace it.

While I called for a tow, my husband researched the source of the problem. He called back after finding a YouTube video with the same symptoms and a possible solution, but he would need to find an auto parts store.

I told him no worries. The van had broken down just outside Joe's Auto Parts. He laughed in disbelief. "You must be kidding," he said, to which I quickly told him, "No kidding!"

I asked him to describe the parts we needed. Instead, he took Joe's address and called the store to see if they had what we needed. Sure enough, they had the parts in stock!

By then the tow truck had arrived. The attendant thought I was crazy when I asked to be towed to our home and seemed to be in such a good mood. He gently asked if we were confident in our ability to fix the vehicle ourselves.

With minimal confidence but a lot of trust, I squeaked out a yes. Then he politely asked why I seemed so happy. I quickly explained that had I broken down just the day before I would have been in minus-30-degree temperatures. He quickly understood and agreed that this was turning out to be a blessing.

My husband and I shared our amazement and, yes, I will say the JOY we experienced in this experience. You see, not only was the weather sixty degrees warmer than the day before, but I was protected and guided to a place where I could get the help I needed. We both knew that with God's provision we would be able to get our vehicle fixed and back on the road.

While it had taken a couple of hours and lots of giggles about our naiveté around auto repairs, I am happy to announce we (the *royal* we—meaning mostly my husband) fixed our van. My lesson was to invite God into my tough moments... to go to Him first and place my trust in Him. He gives us exactly what we need, exactly when we need it. The rest is up to us.

Sarah's Small Act Done with Great Love at Target

As I was explaining to my friend Robin that I was writing a book about where God shows up in the ordinary, she quickly began to share a story about her mentoring experience with a confirmation student at her church and how God showed up in Target. The confirmation students were charged with finding God in the world around them. So where did her student want to go? Well, nowhere else but Target. While dubious at first, but a faithful and loving mentor, Robin went along with it. The students were given a small budget to use in helping someone else.

On the day of her 'research', the student and a fellow confirmation classmate arrived at Target with my friend and another mentor. The students asked if they could explore the store 'solo' to find

God in action. Dear Robin and the other mentor reluctantly agreed and asked the students to meet in the coffee shop a little later to report what they had learned.

The mentor was not surprised to learn the students did not have much luck in their shopping observations. But a stern-faced store security guard seated several tables away from the group suddenly shared a friendly smile before heading over to the front of the store, leaving her cold drink on the table. Apparently the security guard was needed to escort a shoplifter out of the store.

The guard came back to retrieve her drink and began talking to the clerk, the confirmation students and the mentors. She explained how difficult it was to remove a shoplifter and press charges when so many people were taking just what they needed to survive. She said her job was difficult because it involved interacting with people who didn't get enough to eat or were burdened with mental health issues.

The security guard had the students' undivided attention. They were learning about people who lived in their neighborhood who were struggling. They were learning about how issues and actions that seemed black and white sometimes weren't. They were seeing compassion and empathy from a security guard who at first glance appeared to be all about the rules.

This struck a chord with the students. They observed the issue and the security guard's interaction, but no one said anything. Was God somehow in action here?

The students had an idea and asked if they could use their funds to pay forward. or prepay, a drink for the next guest at the coffee shop. What would unconditional generosity look like and what impact might it have? When the clerk learned of the girls' idea, she asked if instead of offering a free drink to one customer, she could give a big discount to several customers. The students loved the idea and went back to the table to watch in delight.

What happened next was the biggest surprise for both the students and the mentors. After seeing several customers enjoy the benefits of the students' pay-it-forward endeavor, the clerk at the register came over to chat. The students had noticed that the clerk's mood seemed joyful. The clerk told the girls that their generosity had touched her deeply. The students and mentors saw a sparkle emerge in this clerk's expression. A renewed sense of service had happened for one who delivers the gift of hospitality to many people every single day.

When the students had decided to pay-it-forward, they had not thought about the impact on the woman behind the counter. They were so focused on the customer they never considered the server and clerk. The clerk went on to share that sometimes her job in food service could be hard. She talked about her faith, her experience of working in a public place—in fact, she shared a lot.

The mentors and students were all amazed for different reasons. The mentors were thrilled that the students had the opportunity to see the Holy Spirit at work. The students were confident that while God wasn't in merchandising, He was alive and active in the hearts and souls of those inside the store. Everyone walked away from the experience understanding that when we make time and space for the holy and sacred, we should be ready for life-changing moments that broaden our understanding of humanity and the spiritual. Most importantly, when we feel called to take action, we may think we know the impact of that action. But in reality the unintended blessing may be outcomes that we never considered. Amen!

Let Your Light Shine

When I first relocated to the Twin Cities, I was blessed to attend Westminster Presbyterian Church. I felt so lucky to join a congregation that embraced me and eased my transition to Minnesota. My time there as a member occurred during a pastoral transition. The congregation had called upon the services of an interim pastor. When Rev. Dan Little came to the pulpit for the first time he mentioned his time as a pastor in the Pittsburgh area.

My ears immediately perked up!

I quickly phoned my dad and grandmother, who are both Pittsburgh natives, and asked them about Rev. Little. Sure enough, he had served in churches where my grandparents were active as officers in the church.

The very next Sunday I walked up to Rev. Little and asked him if he recalled Paul & Winnie from Pittsburgh Pennsylvania. The Reverend looked me right in the eyes and said, "Paul—you mean *elder* Paul?" Yes I responded, that was my grandfather. We were both delighted with our new connection.

Even though I was almost one thousand miles away from home, I felt like I was with family the Sundays Rev. Little was in the pulpit. As I served on committees and had the opportunity to be around him, we found ample opportunities to swap stories. He was remarkably supportive of me during this tender time and I am still fond of those warm memories.

Within a year the church's pastoral recommendation committee had done its work and a new senior pastor was to be called. This meant that the interim pastor's stint would soon be completed. A celebration was planned to thank Rev. Little for his support during the staff transition. On his last Sunday everyone in the congregation waited patiently in line to thank Rev. Little for his service. I was practicing in my head what I would say. How could I thank him in a few meaningful words and moments?

To my surprise, when I got to the front of the line to shake his hand, he gestured for me to come close and whispered in my ear. "Heather, you shine a beautiful light wherever you go. You are a breath of fresh air. Don't let anyone blow out your light. Promise me you will let your light shine."

Tears formed in my eyes. What an amazingly encouraging divine message! I could feel my spirit and soul lift as his words soaked into my being. Such affirmation and warm words from someone who knew my granddaddy! God had covered me that day for my journey.

To this day, when the winds blow and I feel my light being tested, I remember Rev. Little's words with great fondness. I also make sure that when conducting workshops or working with children and adults, I share this message: *You are beautifully made. Let your unique and beautiful light shine.*

Amen!

Obscured

Driving home one day I saw the most astonishing image in the sky. Toward the western horizon the sun was obscured by a huge cloud with beautiful rays of sunshine shooting over the edges. I could only see glimpses of the powerful sun that was behind this immense cloud.

The brilliant, unfolding scene in the sky caused me to think about our human desire to see and know everything about the God who made us. As humans, we do not like mysteries. We seek to prove, dissect and command everything around us. Especially when it comes to faith, many of us need proof. We want to see evidence.

Yet the truth is that we cannot see or even begin to understand our God. Just like the sun hidden behind the clouds above, God remains hidden to us while the emanations of his glory are abundantly clear. While we see God's amazing beauty and power around us, we seek to understand and know all. But that is not for us to do. God intends for some things to be a mystery and calls upon us to trust in Him. We must trust in what we are allowed to know and wait for the beautiful glimpses that are provided us when we see them in our daily lives.

Please consider this an invitation to take the time to see the extraordinary in the ordinary because our Heavenly Father loves us like crazy. When we are connected to Him he gives us fuel for our journeys. He gives us more than we will ever need. Just like the sun being obscured behind that beautiful cloud, our Heavenly Father constantly gives us His unconditional love.

Trust in Him.

Weaving It Together

Some of my most poignant memories are from when I would go with my daddy to visit those who were near the end of their lives. While most of them eventually came to find peace in their journey, I still recall many who wrestled with the choices of how they had lived their lives. Many had spent way too much time in the office, and many others wished they could have seen more of the Divine in their everyday lives, as they did now at the end of their journey.

My hope is that my stories will inspire you to slow down and become more aware of the world around you. It is so important to see a higher power at play in everyday life.

Like Moses, I hope that you will slow down and turn your head to see the burning bush. With the knowledge that you are part of something bigger than you, and being content with what you have been given, you will find that your choices in life will start to change. You will more fully appreciate the importance of being spiritual and learn to let go of the fears and insecurities that hold you back. You will begin to live the life that your Maker wishes for you.

I hope you will live your life with God at the center of it—a life where you can shine His loving light through you. It is truly amazing to see what happens when His light shines into the dark places of your own heart and the hearts of others. Your light may be the only light some people ever get to experience. Don't miss the chance to shine.

So be more aware of what is around you. Open your eyes to the Divine. Let your light shine and live the life that God has in mind for you.

Spending Time in God's Love Letter

I first heard that the Bible was God's love letter to us in a Bible study. Since that class many years ago, I still find this to be very profound. No matter what my day brings me, when I am in God's word in God's love letter, He always provides for me. Many times He reveals a truth or promise that stretches my understanding. But every time it is exactly what I need to hear at that very moment.

I encourage you to take baby steps into God's love letter. Spending time with Him is His desire for each of us. Spend time with Him daily if only for a few moments. Maybe before your feet hit the floor after getting out of bed, maybe by saying thanks for the food you eat, or maybe at the end of the day by giving thanks for your blessings and asking forgiveness for the places where you became separated from God. Begin today and go to Him.

I find reading scripture to be very enriching. I try reading different versions of the same scripture to expand my understanding. I read from the New International version (NIV) to the New Revised Standard Version (NRSV), and many others. Try exploring different versions. You will be amazed how the Word speaks to you and fills you with what you will need at that very moment.

Biblegateway.com is a wonderful Internet tool to locate different versions of the Bible. Here are some of my favorite passages from the English Standard Version (ESV).

Psalm 46:10 ESV

Be still, and know that I am God. I will be exalted among the nations, I will be exalted in the earth!

Psalm 139:1 ESV

O Lord, you have searched me and known me!

Psalm 139:2 ESV

You know when I sit down and when I rise up; you discern my thoughts from afar.

Psalm 139:3 ESV

You search out my path and my lying down and are acquainted with all my ways.

Psalm 139:4 ESV

Even before a word is on my tongue, behold, O Lord, you know it altogether.

Psalm 139:5 ESV

You hem me in, behind and before, and lay your hand upon me.

Psalm 131:2-3 ESV

But I have calmed and quieted my soul, like a weaned child with its mother; like a weaned child is my soul within me. O Israel, hope in the Lord from this time forth and forevermore.

Job 6:24 ESV

Teach me, and I will be silent; make me understand how I have gone astray.

Lamentations 3:25-26 ESV

The Lord is good to those who wait for him, to the soul who seeks him.

Lamentations 3:26 ESV

It is good that one should wait quietly for the salvation of the Lord.

Psalm 37:1-2 ESV

Fret not yourself because of evildoers; be not envious of wrongdoers! For they will soon fade like the grass and wither like the green herb.

Psalm 37:3 ESV

Trust in the Lord, and do good; dwell in the land and befriend faithfulness.

Psalm 37:4 ESV

Delight yourself in the Lord, and he will give you the desires of your heart.

Psalm 37:5 ESV

Commit your way to the Lord; trust in him, and he will act.

1 Corinthians 15:52 ESV

In a moment, in the twinkling of an eye, at the last trumpet. For the trumpet will sound, and the dead will be raised imperishable, and we shall be changed.

Philippians 4:1-23 ESV

Therefore, my brothers, whom I love and long for...Rejoice in the Lord always; again I will say, Rejoice.

Revelation 21:5 ESV

And he who was seated on the throne said, "Behold, I am making all things new." Also he said, "Write this down, for these words are trustworthy and true."

Psalm 100:3 ESV

Know that the Lord, he is God! It is he who made us, and we are his; we are his people, and the sheep of his pasture.

Jeremiah 29:11 ESV

For I know the plans I have for you, declares the Lord, plans for welfare and not for evil, to give you a future and a hope.

God loves you like crazy and seeks to be with you. In ways you never thought imaginable, being with Him will cause small and sometimes large shifts in your life. That is what faith development is all about—trusting in the unseen and removing those things that separate you from God. As with the great statue of David, God sees you within a grand slab of marble. Let Him chip away the things that hold you back from being all you were created to be.

Remembering who you are and *whose* you are will always guide you on your great journey.

Faith Try-Its

Commit to trying new faith practices. Try each of them for a week until you find practices that fit best for what you need to connect with God throughout the day. Experts say it takes sixty-six days to learn a new golf swing, so when you try new faith practices give yourself lots of time.

1. Commit to Inviting God into Your Day. Find something that you do throughout the day (for example: at stop signs, when you touch the brakes, when you do dishes, when you are frustrated) and welcome God in every time you do that behavior. Take this moment of having God being with you. What do you notice/sense/see/feel?

2. Commit to Slowing Down to Be with God. Breathe. On your inhale say: "yah". On your exhale say: "weh". Repeat three to five times. After each group try to sense the stilling in yourself. Try to be open to God being with you in this very moment. What do you notice/sense/see/feel?

3. Commit to Being Still with God. *Be Still and Know That I Am* is a prayer I use frequently. It helps to calm me when the world is harried at best.

Begin by saying: "Be still and know that I am God."

Then: "Be still and know that I am."

Then: "Be still and know."

Then: "Be Still."

Then: "Be."

When you come to the word "Be" stay there for a moment. Try to sense the stilling in yourself. Try to be open to God being with you in this very moment. What do you notice/sense/see/feel?

4. Commit to Inviting God into your Stressed Out Moment. Philippians 4:13 is called the "Ten-Finger prayer!" Since the verse has ten words in it, each word is counted out on each one of your fingers. So when you get stressed, instead of counting to ten, remember the ten-finger prayer "I… can… do… all things… through… Christ… who… strengthens… me". What do you notice/sense/see/feel?

5. Commit to Noticing God. With a stronger connection to your self and a larger capacity, you are more open to seeing or noticing God in your day. What do you notice/sense/see/feel?

6. Commit to Practicing Gratitude First. At every meal say a prayer of thanksgiving. Some even do this before going to bed so they can have positive thoughts of gratitude with them throughout the night. This is really a life changing powerful practice! What do you notice/sense/see/feel?

7. Commit to try Beth Moore's *P.R.A.I.S.E.* method prayer: *P*: Praise; *R*: Repentance; *A*: Acknowledge Christ died to wash away my sins; *I*: Intercessory; *S*: Self—enjoy this time with God; *E*: Equip for your day. I pray this prayer with my children and myself every night. I love the conversations that this prayer starts and the guide for myself and my children. Beth Moore's prayer beautifully helps you to dwell with God and give thanks, repent where you are separated from God, acknowledge that Christ died for us and then takes you into prayer for others and yourself. If you are seeking a daily prayer this a terrific one that I highly recommend to you!

8. Commit to Journaling. Make time every day to jot down what and where you are noticing God in your day. Do you see God in yourself? Do you see God in others? What do you notice/sense/see/feel?

9. Commit to Inviting and Sharing: One of the most powerful practices is inviting others into Seeing and Noticing God. I love to do this with my children. Think about those closest and in a high trust relationship with you, then invite them to share one of the faith practices you have been trying. What do you notice/sense/see/feel?

10. Commit to Being Creative in Prayer and Worship. Try talking to God, praying to God, or being with Him through dance, song, painting, pottery—you name it. Engaging your whole body and heart always has been extremely powerful for the faithful. By shifting how you connect, you may be able to experience a new level of connection. Whatever and wherever you experience and feel joy or peace or love, I would point to God and know that He is close to you. Call upon Him in those moments and invite God into that space, place and activity. What do you notice/sense/see/feel?

Closing Prayer: Bless, Release, Call to Action

This closing prayer is from a letter written by the Apostle Paul to support a faith community he helped start ten years prior in Ephesus. He wanted to encourage the faithful to deepen their relationship with their Heavenly Father even though he was far away in prison.

Ephesians 3:14-21 ESV

For this reason I bow my knees before the Father, from whom every family in heaven and on earth is named, that according to the riches of his glory he may grant you to be strengthened with power through his Spirit in your inner being, so that Christ may dwell in your hearts through faith—that you, being rooted and grounded in love, may have strength to comprehend with all the saints what is the breadth and length and height and depth, and to know the love of Christ that surpasses knowledge, that you may be filled with all the fullness of God.

Now to Him who is able to do far more abundantly than all that we ask or think, according to the power at work within us, to him be glory in the church and in Christ Jesus throughout all generations, forever and ever.

Amen.

Wishing you peace, love and hope as you continue on your faith journey,
Heather

Made in the USA
Lexington, KY
29 November 2017